GENTLEMAN DRUNK

BY

JEFFREY

God Bless

To order your own personal copy please visit
http://agentlemandrunk.com

First edition: July, 2004

Taylor, Jeffrey
A Gentleman Drunk

0-9727047-1-X

1. Taylor, Jeffrey
2. Alcoholism
3. Alcoholic
4. Title

*"I think any alcoholic that reads this story will relate.
I cried. I laughed. I felt what Jeffrey felt.
Jeffrey's story proves one does not have to lose
everything to hit a bottom.
Jeffrey's story is not unlike your story or mine.
Good job, Jeffrey."*

Your friend and sponsor,

Don B.

ACKNOWLEDGMENTS

Special thanks to:

Toby T
Jane S., editor
Fernanda and her graphics team at TheNetMenCorp
Jonathan Gullery in pre-production
Ron Pramschufer and Denise Puryear
at RJ Communications

Dr. Ron Bland of New York and
Dr. Jamie Longe of Salt Lake
for their medical and spiritual guidance

And a very special thanks to my friends at the Back Street
Club in Bountiful, UT.

Chapter 1
(1951-1969)

GROWING UP IN NEW JERSEY

Where do I begin? It's hard to remember. I know I've blocked out a lot. My therapist tells me that I do not want to remember because it hurts too much.

I was born in 1951, and my sister was born in 1953. We grew up in a New Jersey suburb made up mostly of Jewish families. I remember Dad telling me that he changed our family name because he thought people discriminated against Jews.

In order to prove himself, Dad raised money from his Wall Street friends and built one of our town's first temples to accommodate the Jews moving out of Newark. As they escaped "urban" flight, they would find a brand new temple and be introduced to my father. He made a lot of new friends who would eventually become his clients.

I remember having to attend Hebrew school after regular school on Tuesdays and Thursdays from 4-6 and on Sunday mornings from 9-11. I felt isolated from the rest of the public school children and could not understand why I needed to learn Jewish history, culture, and language. The building was always cold during the winter and hot during the summer. I hated myself and gorged on chocolate cookies, cakes, and pies.

I had to go to temple on the two holiest days—Rosh Hashanah and Yom Kippur—and had to fast for an entire day. I saw a lot of people in temple who never were there at any other time of the year. I used to call them "2-day Jews."

When I was 9 years old, I went to a Jewish summer camp in Pennsylvania. I remember having to write to my parents and then wait anxiously for a postcard from a new and distant city. My parents went to Europe on vacation, show up on Visiting Day, and shower me with presents from all over the world.

When I was 11 years old, Dad asked me to go on a trip with him. I remember sitting with my face glued to the left window as the pilot turned on the twin propellers. We flew to Detroit to pack up Grandma's household goods and ship them back East. I remember meeting Grandma a few times but not really getting to know her. Later that year, Grandma died. I remember Dad telling me to wear sunglasses at her funeral. He told me that "gentlemen" do not cry, especially in front of family and business people.

In order to get closer to Grandma, I started to play her piano. I remember practicing the piano during television commercials (I used to watch a lot of TV and get fat). I would then fake out my piano teacher by telling him that I had practiced for hours. I had enough talent to fake out everyone, including my parents, who were never home. And when they were home, they always yelled at each other.

I won my first piano recital with my own compositions. I beat out other students who were older than me and still remember the applause. I fantasized about being famous, bowing many times like TV performers. Yet I never smiled or looked up at anyone.

I started drinking in 1963, at the age of 12, one year

before my Bar Mitzvah. I do not know why. As part of my alcoholic recovery, I have tried to remember first events that have impacted me my entire life. I am now 52 years old, and if I do not figure them out soon, I will probably die a drunk.

I first tasted alcohol after breaking into dad's liquor cabinet with a key I had found on top of the hi-fi cabinet. I remember hating alcohol but still wanting it. I saw my parent's friends drink a lot and wanted what they had — a world that was powerful, exciting, and romantic. Instead, I puked my brains out and had to clean up the place before my parents got home.

My mother would always scream at the household help, accusing them of stealing from the liquor cabinet. The help would always say that they didn't do it. No one ever suspected that I was the criminal. I just watched on the sidelines as maid after maid would get fired for stealing. Did I feel guilty? Never—it was my little secret.

I hated living. I was fat and ugly. My sister had all the friends and lovers. My father commuted to Wall Street and made lots of money for lots of people, while Mom spent a lot of time at the club playing the company wife. Everyone, including my father and mother, thought we had the perfect family. The only problem was that I was miserable, and no one could tell. I thought my parents could see it on my face. But they never did.

Every weekend, we would be invited to parties. It was always someone's graduation or someone's Bar/Bas Mitzvah. I saw people drink at funerals. I was surrounded by suburban wealth, and I couldn't wait to get out of my home. I hated living and often thought of killing myself. I was attracted to other people who also wanted to kill themselves. At night, I would sneak out of my second floor bedroom window and sit on the roof and stare at the stars. I would talk to myself and pretend that I would be happy one day. That feeling lasted for seconds and then reality would set in. I hated myself, and I thought of jumping off the roof many times.

Often, I would walk down the street in the early morning hours, sit in my neighbors' yards, and stare through their windows. I wanted another life, and I did not know how to get it. One time, I was busted by the police who brought me home in my pajamas. My sister had told my parents that I was missing. When the police found me, I pretended to be "sleepwalking."

One day one of the town bullies came over to our house and picked a fight with me. The other kids in the neighborhood came over to find us fighting. After a quick battle, I went inside, embarrassed and ashamed of losing. My mother told me that Dad would deal with me when he got home. Later that night, I told Dad that I wanted to learn how to defend myself. He told me that "gentlemen" do not fight, and I grew up getting the crap beat out of me.

My parents knew they had a problem child but did not know what to do with me. They told me that I needed to go to a private boys school to help me get into a good university. I told them I did not want to go away. They told me that I was going, so I failed the entrance exam. Dad made a sizeable contribution, and I was in.

Because my father got up very early to get to the city, and my mother preferred sleeping, I had to walk over a mile to town to catch the bus. The bullies on the bus would beat me up often. And no one did anything about it. Eventually, I stopped telling people and kept to myself. I cried when I was alone, and no one seemed to care. Not even my parents.

I began to drink more and more, and I prayed that I would never get caught. I wanted to drown my troubles. I did not know what else to do.

My school troubles continued. I was frequently knocked down by older students in the hallway or stuffed into a hall closet. Often I would hang out with the other "losers" in the chess, audio visual, or music clubs. It was now 1964, and cool people joined high school sororities, athletic teams, or junior achievement.

Instead, I watched life go by and wanted to hurt people. I would keep a list of people I wanted to get even with—teachers, classmates, parents, sister. I wanted to make their lives as miserable as mine. Unfortunately, I never said a word because I learned early in life that no one cared.

On weekends, I would attend "teen corners" at the local junior high school. I would sit alone and drink a Coke while I fantasized about breaking, once again, into my father's liquor cabinet. Eventually, I met a group of people called "hoods," and I started spending time with them. They all had access to their parents' liquor cabinet and to their cigarettes.

When I was 15 years old, I got a phone call from a friend who asked me to come over to his house and have sex with a girl. When I arrived, my friends were drinking beer. I was told that in order to join their club I had to have sex with this girl. I still remember seeing the girl drinking herself silly with the guys groping and sucking her breasts. I was so sick from the scene that I threw up in their backyard. When these "friends" found out, I was never invited back.

To make some money, I caddied for women at the country club. All of the women wore short skirts to show off their legs and their bodies. I made a lot of money and learned a lot about lousy husbands. I fantasized about having sex with all of the women, but nothing ever happened.

For the next few years, I spent more and more time by myself. Dad was a rising star on Wall Street and kept making more and more money. At age 17, Dad told me that he would buy me a car for passing my driver's test. Since he never spent time with me, I was surprised.

I remember that one Saturday getting into Dad's car and driving to the showroom. We walked through the parking lot and he told me to pick whatever car I wanted. Dad told me that he would pay for the car and the yearly insurance. All I had to do was pay for gasoline and maintenance. I wanted to drive and show him my accomplishment. He told me that he did not have the time and that my driving would make him nervous.

I would drive my new car to school every day. However, my so-called "friends" would sneak out to my car and put stones in the hubcaps. I would hear the noise when I started to drive, and they would be standing around the corner laughing their heads off. One time, I took out a crowbar from the car and lunged after them until I fell down, exhausted and humiliated.

When I was a junior in high school, I went out for the wrestling team. I wanted to do something that would make people notice me. My first-year-record was 4 and 10.

My parents reluctantly came to the School's annual talent show. Everyone would applaud while I watched my family sitting there feeling anxious and uncomfortable. I never knew why they could not enjoy my success.

My parents entertained a lot. Every weekend, the house would be filled with Wall Street big shots. My parents would talk about their problems while I hung around the kitchen with the catered help. I learned about life through the caterer's eyes. I was not allowed to sample food or to eat until I played the piano for my parents and their friends. At the appropriate time, I would be called into the living room to perform. I clearly remember everyone quieting down and getting their seats, while Dad made another predictable announcement of how proud he was of me. Not once did he ever say that directly to me.

I would always play the same two songs—"Autumn Leaves" and the "Theme from Exodus." I was in my moment for those short 6 minutes. I would never look at people, only at my piano. I never needed sheet music because I could remember every note and would improvise, as necessary, to get the biggest applause. I still remember my endings. I would always do a dramatic pause, a thundering crescendo, and then a powerful glissando. There would be 3-5 seconds of silence while I rose from the parquet bench, put my left hand on the side of the piano, and bowed. The sound of applause would last in my head for minutes.

Then, instead of meeting the people, my parents would shove me back into the kitchen so they could hustle the group. It was only after the performance that I would get to eat some dinner in the kitchen with the caterers.

My sister always ate in her room by herself. She was exempt from dinner because she was a girl and younger.

Being a man, I had to wait for dad to come home, exhausted and tired from his long day at the office. I would eat in silence while my parents ate in silence or yelled and screamed at each other.

To get our attention, Mom would often try to kill herself with drug overdoses from the medicine cabinet. Dad always called the doctor for help, while I walked Mom around the room to prevent her from falling asleep and possibly dying.

I could legally drink at age 18, and I took full advantage of it. I found every bar in New Jersey and New York that would take me. I had the money and would buy drinks for myself and anyone else who was willing to listen to me.

At the senior prom, my friend got drunk, and I stole his date. We went down the shore and drank on the beach with booze that I had in my little red convertible. I remember making out on the beach and passing out. When we awoke at 2:00 in the morning, I drove her home and got yelled at by her parents.

When I had the chance to get away, I did. It was 1969. I went away to college and swore I would never return to my birthplace.

Chapter 2
(1969-1975)

WILD CAMPUS DAYS

From 1969 to 1973, I went to school in St. Louis, except for my junior year when I studied music in France. I had applied to many undergraduate schools and got accepted to most of them. Dad wanted me to go to Harvard, but I refused to apply.

In the spring of 1969, Dad and I flew to St. Louis to my school of choice. I was excited and motivated because the university wanted more students from the Northeast – something to give them more nationwide recognition.

Cherry blossoms and girls dominated the quadrangle. Having attended an all-boys school for 5 years, I needed to get a life, or I would literally explode. I knew nothing about dating, let alone social etiquette, and I wanted to sample as many girls as possible.

I remember Mom and Dad sending me off in September 1969. I do not remember either of them crying. I remember just wanting to leave New Jersey and get on my second-ever flight to my new home.

The school picked up the freshmen at the airport for the short ride to campus. I was assigned a roommate in an all-boys dorm. My roommate wanted to pledge a fraternity and encouraged me to join him. My father told me that I should pledge his fraternity, and that they would have to take the son of a "legacy."

Pledging was difficult. I remember sitting on a large block of ice for hours. I remember having to strip down, tie a string to my penis, tie the other end of the string to a napkin holder, and hand the napkin holder to another pledge standing next to me, who was drunk.

The fraternity brothers drank up a storm and threw empty beer bottles around the room. I could hear the crashing sound but could not see anything since all pledges were blindfolded.

The pledge master told us that in order to get into the fraternity we would have to show our trust in our pledge brothers. I felt my pledge brother, who was holding my string, swaying to and fro. Suddenly, the pledge master told us to throw the napkin holders. I couldn't do it, and I knew that I would fail the initiation. Of course, my drunken pledge brother threw the napkin holder and broke a window. I fell to the floor thinking I was going to lose my dick. God must have intervened since the weight of the napkin holder broke the string.

Everyone laughed while I cried. Nonetheless, I became a fraternity man who wore his fraternity pin and sweater all the time. I was now powerful and wanted people to know it.

I remember my first fraternity party. Liquor flowed all over the place. People would get drunk and steal into someone's bedroom to have sex. It was the year of the Aquarius, and free love was rampant. No one thought of condoms or safe sex. Everyone was encouraged to try anything. Drugs were plentiful and dealers would hang around the fraternity house. Money was everywhere so no one went without.

I was a virgin and nervous about getting laid for the first time. On my journey to love, I indulged in a high-powered combination of Everclear alcohol and grape juice, commonly known as "Purple Passion." Unfortunately, nothing ever happened, and all I did was talk to girls who were upset with their boyfriends. I quickly developed a reputation as the "guy that people could go to solve their problems."

In the spring my roommate locked me in a room with two other fraternity brothers. They told me that I was too uptight, and that I needed to get stoned.

It took me several weeks to feel the impact of the marijuana. It relaxed me, and I wanted more. The local dealer hung around the fraternity house and I scored my first lid for $35.

I loved smoking and drinking. The combination was powerful, and I felt part of the group. I would get more dates, and we would get stoned in my convertible. Being a budding businessman, I started to sell drugs to friends and bought volume at wholesale prices. I remember doing deals in the back of my dealer's car in the local public park. I would drive down to the park at 2:00 a.m. and flash my headlights, just like in the movies. I felt powerful and cool. I never had to pay for marijuana again—always took my percentage off the top.

Once in a while, we would score great stuff from Mexico or Hawaii. Occasionally, a truckload of hashish would come in from Germany. I never did anything more powerful.

My fraternity brothers, especially the pre-med students, would take more powerful pills such as Methedrine or Mescaline. One of them stood at a traffic light for an hour before I noticed that he did not move. I had to go out and escort him to campus.

At the end of my freshman year, several students were killed at Kent State and two of our dormitories were bombed. Since the dean did not want any trouble, he sent us home without taking our final exams. We were given P for passing or F for failing.

At the same time, the U.S. government implemented a lottery system for the draft. With classes cancelled, we attended rallies, made love in the afternoon, smoked our brains out, and drank as if there were no tomorrow. I pulled a high draft number and felt relief. One of my college friends, who pulled a low draft number, killed himself. Several of my neighbors back home also killed themselves through accidental overdoses. Many low number friends fled to Canada to avoid the draft. Few of my friends actually served.

Two years passed quickly. As a music major, I was able to study in France. It was there that I learned a lot about cheap French wines. Everyone there drank and if you didn't, you were considered unsociable.

Since I could converse fluently in French, I would be invited to people's homes for dinner. As a reward, I would play their often out-of-tune pianos. I learned French music and sampled homemade French pre-dinner and after-dinner drinks.

I would only date American girls since the French girls did not shave their armpits or legs in those days. They learned that from their mothers in World War II.

My senior year was marked with more drinking parties as I started to hang around drama and music students. As pledge chairman for my fraternity, I would run Purple Passion parties and invite everyone I knew.

As I began to write musicals, school studies became secondary. I would buy doughnuts at the local bakery at 5:00 a.m. and hustle them at the library in order to make money for gas and drinks.

My father convinced me to take a computer course and I learned COBOL, which the U.S. government was pushing on American businesses, and FORTRAN, which was used in universities to develop models.

Each summer, I would go back to summer camp in Pennsylvania and drive other counselors to New York for drinking sprees. My favorite drink was Whiskey Sour, which was expensive. My friends drank cheap wine like Annie Green Springs or Boone's Farm. It was at summer camp that I had my first sex with a cheerleader from Texas in the backseat of my convertible. I remember almost putting my foot through the back window as I yelled, "Oh My God!"

After five years at private school and four years at college, I was tired. I remember telling Dad that I wanted to drop out of school to "find myself." He said "Fine" but he would cut me off financially. Hearing that, I decided to go to graduate school. I wanted to study drama at Northwestern but got turned down. Instead, I attended a well-known business school in downtown Chicago.

For two years, I worked my tail off and hated life. Unlike my under graduate college days, where I was happy most of the time, I was reintroduced to a world that I did not like. Most graduate students hated each other and they, literally, would stab you in the back or kill to get a first-round interview with a major corporation. Corporations would come to campus and sponsor "Liquidity Preference Parties" to aspiring MBA candidates. To drown my sorrows, I worked nightly at the student computer center and wasted my earnings on drinks and dope.

Since I found school boring, I started the Graduate School Follies, a musical parody. My friends and I had a difficult time recruiting students to participate because they were either into their studies or afraid of getting yelled at by the professors we planned to mock.

Like high school, I couldn't wait to graduate. But my grades were low, and the dean put me on probation. As God would have it, one of my professors took a liking to me and helped coach me to pass my orals. This professor eventually went on to become the dean of the graduate school of business.

A major East Coast bank heard about my newly-discovered computer modeling skills and asked me to work in New York City for a summer. Having survived that trial by fire, I was offered a full-time job.

Chapter 3
(1975-1984)

PARTY TIME IN NEW YORK CITY AND SAN FRANCISCO

I am now 24 years old with a freshly minted MBA from a top business school. I start working as a systems officer making $18,000 a year, complete with 4 weeks of vacation. I find a 1-bedroom apartment on the Upper East Side of New York City. I have arrived.

But I have no real social life. I work 70 hours a week and practically live at the bank's Data Center on Wall Street.

At the end of every day, I head over to Rosie O'Gradys, the local bar, and hang out with fellow bank officers. I learn about scotch, and I fall in love with it. The wonderful liquid goes down so smoothly, and it is so sophisticated. On weekends, I hang around Caliente Cab Company down in the village where they serve a mean margarita.

Two years pass, and I am on the road to financial success. My boss loves me, and his boss loves my boss, so we all get along. While my MBA friends struggle to get ahead uptown in the corporate finance or M&A areas, I quickly get promoted for designing systems to eliminate blue collar workers.

Over time, loneliness scares me and I start to drink more heavily. Although I meet women at bars, I do not like the scene. My friends try to fix me up on dates but nothing seems to work. I sleep around with strangers and never worry about the consequences.

One day I go out with Honora who works for my father. After several dates, I ask her to marry me. Unfortunately, I confuse sex/lust with love, and our engagement fails miserably. I remember my parents' rage and embarrassment because the wedding invitations had already gone out.

To drown my sorrows, I throw a party and provide all the dope and liquor. To ensure its success, and get a fresh batch of dates, I ask every woman to bring another woman.

Approximately 150 people show up at my 1-bedroom apartment. So we move the party to the hallway and party till dawn. That evening I talk to Lizzann, who I learn works at the same bank. We date several times and stay at my place on the East Side or at her place on the West Side. Often we would go to work together in yesterday's clothes.

At work, I discover that my employer is parking foreign exchange trading profits in Nassau to minimize U.S. taxes. Although not illegal, I feel uncomfortable. I share my discovery with my boss who, surprisingly, offers me an all expense-paid relocation to San Francisco.

Clumsily, I tell Lizzann that I do not love her and cannot promise anything. But I offer her the opportunity to join me in California. Since Lizzann works for the same bank, they tell me that they will help her find a job out there. So, the two of us move to San Francisco.

We attend a lot of parties and smoke a lot of great dope, chasing our highs with scotch and fancy-colored drinks. Each Sunday, we brunch, have cracked crab with bloody marys or screwdrivers, and end the day with a walk over to Ghirardelli Square for hot fudge sundaes.

Lizzann and I marry in June 1978 in Sausalito on top of the mountain. We hire a great jazz band and throw a party that people talked about for years. We save up enough money to buy a house in Corte Madera. I commute to San Francisco on the Larkspur Ferry after riding my bike to the terminal. On weekends and holidays, we entertain lots of naked people in our hot tub, offering unlimited amounts of California-grown weed.

A year later our employer asks us to move back to New York. At the time, my wife was in grad school, and I did not want to go back. So I quit my job and retained a recruiter who got me into a Big 8 consulting practice.

For two years I traveled and developed a nationwide minicomputer hardware and software selection business practice. On the largest projects, I would live on the road for two weeks and return home for a short weekend. The company paid me hardship duty and put me up in the best hotels.

At the end of every day, the project teams would down cocktails and at least two bottles of wine. I then refocused my drinking energies on wine instead of liquor. It felt more mature, sophisticated, and elegant.

When I was in town, Lizzann and I would go to the wine country and buy cases of Merlot and Cabernet from the nearby Napa Valley vineyards.

Our first child, Jordana, was born in March 1983. My parents flew out to see their new grandchild, and I remember yelling at my parents when they offered me advice on how to raise Jordana. I still have the video of my mother crying on the sofa as I took my daughter out of her arms.

By 1984, I was making a lot of money with my Big 8

employer and was 1-2 years away from the partnership. I remember being invited to a partner's home for a party and witnessed several partners grabbing women in all of the wrong places. Booze flowed freely, and secretaries saw their chance to move into the consulting ranks by being extremely nice to senior managers.

The whole scene disgusted me, and I started blowing my chances to become a partner. I would start arguing with partners, second-guessing their decisions, and sitting in their offices when they were out of town.

Nonetheless, fate intervened. I was offered an opportunity to take my equipment leasing skills, which I had learned on the job, and apply them to two clients in Charlotte, North Carolina. Since no one else had the skill set that I had, and since no else wanted to transfer to Charlotte, the company offered me a compensation package that was breathtaking.

Chapter 4
(1984-1987)

JORDANA, MOIRA AND DIVORCE

Short-term computer consulting projects stretch from one day to one month to one year and beyond. They never stop because clients keep asking for more features to be added to their new systems. In order to balance my work and home life, I commute to Charlotte to service my bank clients while my wife raises our 1-year-old daughter back in California.

I'm working 10-hour days, 7 days a week, and drink at night to forget my existence. It was in North Carolina that I learned about Southern Comfort, which reminded me of scotch. Southern Comfort became my drink of choice because it seemed more gentlemanly and sophisticated to say, "I'll have a Southern Comfort on the rocks." The drink went down smoothly, warmly, and gently—just like a warm Southern night.

After several years of marriage, Lizzann and I start arguing about my weekly long distance travel. To save our marriage meant that either she or I would have to sacrifice. Being the man (remember that it's the early 1980s), meant that I got 90% of the vote. So we sold our home in Corte Madera and bought a lake home in Charlotte.

The money continued to flow, my drinking progressed, and I began to smoke a stronger brand of locally-grown marijuana. Life was good, and I could not complain. I would take Jordana for rowboat rides on our lake, and I can still remember asking her; "where's your ear, where's your eyes, where's your tush?" In answer to my last question, she would look at me quizzically and put her hands on her backside. I still have it on video.

Two years after Jordana's birth, Lizzann and I talk about having a second child. I tell her that I am not ready, and that I need more time to think about it. Lizzann argues that if we wait too long, it will be harder and that Jordana needs to have a brother or sister. I think about my father, who was an only child, and agree with her. Nonetheless, I am angry.

I become disenchanted with Charlotte, hate the people I socialize with on weekends, and escalate my fights. My drinking progresses, and I begin to yell and scream at people for no apparent reason. I begin to embarrass Lizzann in public, and we start to drift apart.

To complicate matters, California management is not happy with the fact that I am giving advice to clients which contradicts their advice. As a result, I begin to compromise my morals and drink more frequently to compensate for the quagmire in which I live.

In late 1985, I throw away my last chance at the partnership and tell my wife that I want to form my own company. Lizzann tells me that I am destroying our marriage. I tell her that I cannot continue to fly back and forth to San Francisco, support the house in Charlotte, spend substantial time with my daughter, and give her the time that she thinks she deserves.

Reluctantly, Lizzann agrees. I turn in my notice, cash in my deferred savings, and borrow against our Charlotte home. With those funds, I form a company to develop training software on a newly announced IBM XT.

Time goes by, and I become exceedingly depressed. Although I spend more time at home, my brain spends every available moment with my software while my heart indulges in drink and drug.

I travel around the country to find clients for my company. As things go from bad to worse, we decide to have a second child. I begin to pray daily and ask God for help. I fantasize that He will not let me down because He would never want a "hero" to lose. At one point, I think about killing myself. You know the fantasy—where everyone cries at your death and the insurance company takes care of the survivors. While I am crying hysterically in my hotel room, I have the sense to call my father for help. I remember him yelling that I was stupid for quitting and giving up the partnership. My father tells me to stop crying and get a hold of myself, and that he will wire me some money. He tells me to go out for dinner and take it like a man. To this day, this surrealistic episode reminds me of a poorly written John Wayne dialogue.

As predicted, my business continues to go downhill, and I miss the birth of Moira, our second daughter. In order to save my business and our marriage, I ask Lizzann to move with me to New Jersey where I think I can land some business. She says no and tells me that she does not want to have anything to do with me.

Upon returning home from a road trip, Lizzann hands me my walking papers. I cry hysterically—my business is failing, I am responsible for two young children, a home mortgage that I cannot afford, and a second loan secured for my business.

We are forced to sell the house and pay off the loans. Lizzann moves to another home in Charlotte while I go back to New York to find work. Of course, my father does not want me to wind up on the streets so he allows me to stay in one of his corporate apartments and tries to help me get back on my feet by opening doors with some of his clients. I now look back and realize that my father was doing the best he could to help me; while I could not help myself. Had I known about my drinking problem then, and gotten help in a formal recovery program, who knows what I might have been able to do with my life.

So I pack my few belongings, ship my 1898 concert grand Bechstein, and move back to New York. For several months, I work at different jobs. I continue to smoke and drink. Monday night becomes my favorite drinking night for the low- price drink specials. From time to time, I play piano at various bars in order to make some more money to pay off my debts. Dad continues to throw his frustrations at me howling that I wasted my life.

I fly back and forth to North Carolina every four weeks to see my kids. Sadly, Lizzann makes me wait outside for the kids, never being asked to come inside. I take the girls to the Holiday Inn, which has an enclosed swimming pool, watch them swim for hours, and feed them powdered dough-nuts for breakfast. At night when they are asleep, I drink and smoke in the bathroom and try to make the most of it.

I do not know how I survived those years. But, I know that God lit my darkened path. He introduced me to Toby.

Chapter 5
(1987-1993)

TOBY

I leave my soon-to-be ex-wife in Charlotte with our two young children and head straight back to New York. During the day, I make great money and pay off my lenders. At night, I frequent bars and drink myself into oblivion.

My social life sucks. Unfortunately, my friends do not want to introduce me to any women because they know that I am looking to get laid.

After six months, I tell my friend Richie that I'm bored and that I need a break from New York City. Richie tells me that he is a travel agent and that I should go to Club Med Turquoise in the Caribbean. Richie tells me that the women are hot there and that everyone drinks, gets naked and runs around on private secluded beaches for hours—nothing but pure pleasure.

I ask Richie, "How much?" He tells me a couple of thousand and to put it on a credit card. I shake at spending that kind of money and cannot do it.

A week later I go to a graduate school alumni meeting and sit next to an extremely attractive blonde, whom I immediately want. She tells me that she is going to Club Med Turquoise the following week and that I should call her when she gets back.

Watching this miracle unfold, I immediately call Richie

and tell him that I need to get on her plane. He asks me her name. Richie starts to laugh and tells me that he sold her the plane ticket and that I should stay away from her because she's crazy. Denying what I hear, I tell Richie that he wants her for himself.

Knowing that I have to win her over with one glance, I rush over to the nearest clothing store and ask the prettiest clerk to dress me. I tell her to make me look handsome and "fuck the budget." Hindsight says that you should never go into a New York City store and say "fuck the budget." As a result of this impetuous, childlike action, I spend a lot of money to look like Sydney Greenstreet in "Casablanca" by buying an orange shirt, white pants, shoes, belt, and a white Panama hat.

I get to Newark Airport and await the charter to Club Med Turquoise. I do not see the blonde. Instead, I meet Paul, hit it off, and we agree to become roommates at the Club.

I arrive later that afternoon, get dressed, and head over to the bar. I see the blonde and approach from behind. I tap her on the shoulder. She turns and screams "How dare you follow me? Stalker! Stalker!" Everyone begins to look at me. I run to my room, fall on the bed, and cry uncontrollably.

Paul walks into the room and listens to my sob story. In between laughs and total disbelief, he suggests that I get stoned to take away my troubles. He reminds me that there are plenty of women out there who want me. After smoking with him for a couple of minutes, I forget why I am there.

After falling on the floor and realizing the stupidity and ridiculousness of my long-distance fantasy, we go to the Club's disco at the end of the island. Paul sees Eileen, a woman that he met on the plane, and takes me over to say hello.

Eileen introduces Toby, her roommate. I say hello and ask Toby "Did you know that your shirt is inside out?" Toby laughs and tells me that it is made to look that way. We dance the entire evening, kiss goodnight, and I'm in love again.

The next day Toby wakes up, opens her door, and finds me sitting outside anxiously awaiting her appearance. I rise to my feet, apologize profusely for frightening her, and tell her that I just wanted to see her get ready for the day. She thinks I'm crazy, yet lets me into her room.

We spend most of the day together at the nude beach where I had a hard time getting up since I stuck my dick in the sand and was hard from watching all the naked babes parade along the beach. Lesson for the day — never stick your dick in hot sand and let your pride get in the way.

Toby and I see each other nightly. She thinks I am a nuisance and reminds me that I cannot be in love since I hardly know her. I deny her words and profess my love for her like the writer in Moulin Rouge who falls in love with Nicole Kidman. Every time I inform her that we have made beautiful, wonderful love, she laughs and tells me to get a life.

At Club Med, they do not use money. You give them your credit card number back in the States in return for beads (can be exchanged for drinks at the club) which you wear around your neck. Since I wanted people to know I was wealthy, I wore several strands at a time.

When I was not with Toby, I would go over to Lover's Beach and look for beads, which I could turn in for more drinks. Turns out lots of people lost beads at the beach as they made love under the moonlit skies.

I would walk around the beach with my Walkman, lis-

tening to Natalie Cole or Bette Midler, and find lots of beads
which I would attach to my ever-lengthening strands. I was
alone most of the time and enjoyed the peace and quiet,
getting stoned in my room in the morning, spending the
day wandering aimlessly on the beach, and making love to
Toby in the evening. Life was good.

When we get back to New York, I can't stop thinking
about Toby and call her for a date.

Toby lived in Brooklyn and my New York City advisors
(strangers I would meet in bars) discouraged me from seeing her because she was GU (Geographically Undesirable).
Yet, I knew I wanted to see her again. I was fascinated by her
upbringing and the difficulty she had in raising two children
on her own. I kept thinking that if she could handle her difficult life, she could help me with mine.

Toby, on the other hand, told me that I needed therapy
to help me solve my problems, So I started individual therapy with Toby's former therapist. Later, Toby and I did couple and group therapy. Although most of our money went
into therapy, I still had enough left over for drinking, smoking, and partying. In fact, several of the group members par-
tied together when we were not in session.

Our first date was at an Italian restaurant on 39th Street.
I remember watching Toby and thinking that I was not good
enough for her. She was so beautiful, talented, and classy. She
told me about her dancing with the Ballet Russe de Monte
Carlo and how she played the lead in "My Fair Lady" and
"Peter Pan."

On weekends, I would go over to the Broadway ballet
school and watch Toby practice. I would sit still in the corner like a little kid and watch her dance for hours. I could

not keep my eyes off of her. I was in love and kept telling her. She kept telling me that I was in lust and could not be in love since we hardly knew each other.

One night, Toby finally consents to stay over at my apartment. This was a major step for Toby since she had to leave her kids behind.

My apartment is Spartan except for my 1898 concert grand Bechstein. The white walls stand bare since I have no idea how to decorate the place. My therapist suggests that I should decorate the apartment with things that will make me feel good. As much as I think and look for ideas, nothing pops into my head. I keep thinking of Toby, getting stoned and having sex in my single bed next to the grand piano, which takes up the entire apartment.

After dinner that night, I play a song that I had composed the day before for Toby and ask her to sing it. The apartment glowed with her first soprano voice and I could hear an orchestra in my head. To this day, "Two Strangers Meet" is still my favorite song.

Along with the good times were disastrous moments that I now wish never happened. Once I lost it while I was lecturing in San Francisco. Toby and I had a terrible argument, and I hit her directly in the face. I remember her cowering in the corner, frightened and scared. I fell to my knees and cried. I knew that I was out of control. I crawled over to her and promised her that I would never hit her again. To this day, I have never broken that promise.

As I felt more comfortable with our relationship, Toby and I agreed that I should give up my apartment and move in with her in Brooklyn. Although, I was happy with Toby, I was unhappy with the rest of my life.

Toby and I got married on the roof top of my former apartment building 18 months from the day we met. I had always wanted to get married with a skyline view. God did not disappoint anyone who attended our wedding. Everyone was dressed in a tuxedo or evening gown and looked elegant. Toby and I performed and everyone commented that it was more like a show than a wedding. To this day, we still watch the video when we feel like smiling or laughing.

We honeymooned in Hawaii, and I spent most of the time behind the video camera. I felt it was more important to capture the moment so that I could watch it for years. Of course, I missed the opportunity to experience it. I remember waking up one morning, looking at her sleeping quietly in the luxurious king-size bed, going out on the terrace, watching the sun rise on Waikiki Beach, and getting stoned.

I also remember going to a very expensive restaurant and trying to impress Toby with my knowledge of scotch. To show her how cool I am, I order a glass of Blue Label Scotch for $50 a glass. I'm sorry to report that it was not worth the money.

My memories of Brooklyn are still fuzzy. But I do still remember being robbed at knifepoint at 5:00 p.m. while walking back to the apartment from the train station. I remember two guys holding me from behind while the third guy yells at me to give him my wallet. I tell him that he is stupid since I cannot get to my wallet with my hands held behind my back. He tells me to shut up and lie down on the ground. I tell him that if he is going to kill me, I want to see him do it. His friends take my wallet and my briefcase and run across the street. Hours later, Toby sees me in the police car driving around looking for my never-found assailants.

It was this event, along with other smaller ones, that convinced us to cut back on expenses, save money faster, and move out of our rapidly deteriorating neighborhood.

After months of foregoing luxury, we buy a small house, without garage, in Putnam County. I commute to New York City and sleep on the train in both directions. Toby commutes to Brooklyn and spends the majority of the day in her car. At night, we fall asleep exhausted. But we have our house on weekends and party constantly with weekend visitors.

My business life changes when I team up with a man from Utah. He directs one of his associates to fly to New York to interview me and they hire me as a classroom instructor.

My personal life changes when I get a call from Mom. She tells me that while she was away with my sister's son, Dad had a stroke after playing a rigorous round of tennis. We fly to Florida and meet with his surgeon who tells us that Dad has 3-6 months to live. After several years at home, and Dad constantly whistling for Mom's attention, she puts him in a special care facility. To this day, 13 years later, Dad still eats three meals a day and loves ice cream.

For two years, I fly anywhere Sudhir, my Utah boss, wants me to go. Pressure builds up, and I start to drink more and more until I am mixing different drinks in order to sleep better at night. Often I take dope on the road and smoke at night to relax. Nonetheless, no one knows that I drink or smoke because I function well in the classroom; often receiving standing ovations.

At this point, I start to drink on airplanes, drink in airport club rooms, drink at hotel bars, drink at dinner, return to the hotel bar for night caps, and drink mini-bottles in my room late at night while I watch comedies or Tony Robbins infomercials at 2:00 a.m.

At home, my drinking habits start to deteriorate. I begin to scream and get angry at the littlest of things. Deep down inside I feel empty, listless, and without direction.

Chapter 6
(1993-2002)

INTERNATIONAL
ROAD WARRIOR

Several years go by and Sudhir continues to critique my classroom performance. With his guidance, my lectures improve. For several years, I travel in luxury and lecture in Australia, Canada, Hong Kong, Ireland, Italy, Korea, Kuwait, Malta, Mexico, Nigeria, Portugal, and Singapore.

For 200 + days a year, I lecture by day and entertain in the evening, while drinking my way to sleep. Late at night, after the clients fade, I recognize my loneliness and seek companionship at the hotel bar. I hit on a lot of beautiful women, but always pass out before anything ever happens. One time, I wake up with a telephone number written on my hand and cannot remember a thing.

Over time, Sudhir continues to urge us to move to Utah. For a year, he flies me out for business meetings, takes me skiing at Deer Valley, and invites Toby and me to dine with him and his wife. Sudhir keeps comparing Utah to New York and tells me that moving there will improve my life.

Toby and I spend a lot of time arguing and screaming about moving to Utah. For every good reason I can think of to move, she comes up with another one to stay. I argue that it would be good for my business career and she argues that she does not want to give up New York and leave her children. In 1993, IBM announces massive layoffs and the housing market in Putnam County starts to tank.

Sudhir's offer begins to look more attractive, and we decide to move. He gives us a weekend to find housing and, through the strangest luck, buy a house north of the city that we still live in to this day.

My traveling begins to adversely affect Toby. She starts to complain about my not being at home and I can tell that she feels abandoned living in Utah. Instead of making things better, I tell her to stop complaining. Our fights became more vicious.

If business had been better, I could have argued that our lives had improved. Unfortunately, my boss started to give me some lousy assignments and I found myself in such dangerous places as Nigeria. To get into the country, I had to smuggle money in the lining of my ski jacket, using it judiciously for bribes.

Upon leaving Nigeria, they stop me at the border for bribing a guard. I admitted to the officer that he was correct but that the guard had asked for the bribe.

I patiently stand still, looking at my plane, worrying that I will be detained forever. While sweating bullets, the officer asks the guard in his native language to join our conversation.

The officer first looks at my eyes and then at the guard's. He thumbs through my passport and examines my visa. He sees that I have papers inviting me to the country, and that I had met with the prime minister of finance.

I do not know what the officer was thinking. But he politely hands me my papers, tells me "Good Luck" in

English, and escorts me to the plane. I thank him, look back, and see the guard being dragged away by the military.

I take my seat and sob uncontrollably.

One day I work late at the office and decide to take a new way home. It is snowing heavily, and I am driving a very old Vega, which has seen its best days. To my disbelief, as I enter an intersection I get hit by a speeding car coming over a hill, and my car flips over three times. Contrary to popular belief, as you are dying you do not think of your loved ones.

The paramedics arrive and use a blow torch to get me out of my car. They operate on my left ankle and put a steel rod in my leg, which still exists to this day. I have three broken ribs and wear crutches for six weeks.

After a year of brutal domestic and international travel, I learn that my employer has cashed out and sold his company to Euromoney, a British conglomerate. None of the employees get contracts, and we are all suddenly unemployed.

Toby and I find ourselves stranded and worry about choices. Do we stay in Utah? Do I start my own business? Do we move back to New York?

I decide to broker leasing transactions, hang around equity conferences, and hit on people who get turned down for equity finance. I explain to them the benefits of leasing equipment in the interim and secure enough business to keep me alive.

During the day I chase clients and in the evening I down as many double scotches as necessary to put me to sleep.

During this self-pity phase, I meet Allen. Allen is a smooth talker and convinces me to find funding for several of his transactions. Since I want to please him, I work my tail off to prove myself. Yet, every time I get close to making a deal, Allen changes his mind. One day, I stop by his office and learn that the FBI has taken him away. The *Wall Street Journal* announces that Allen has gone to prison for a "pump and dump" penny-stock scheme.

A year later, Euromoney calls me and asks if I would like to help restore their business. After negotiating a decent contract, I work around the clock to undo the damage caused by the merger.

Five years later, Euromoney fires me because I have become too expensive. I sue them for wrongful discharge and win. I take that money and form my next company, which I still operate out of my home.

With newly-found freedom, I increase my consumption of alcohol. Toby and I join several private clubs and frequently attend wine-laden dinners with other well-to-do couples from the Salt Lake City area. We invest in cases of wine, which we ship in illegally from California, to fill each slot of our five wine racks and refrigerators.

I move up to 18-year-old single malt scotch, secure the most expensive tequila that I bring back from my frequent trips to Mexico, and try out local beer in every country that I visit.

I drink before events, during events, and after events, while constantly changing alcohols out of boredom. Often, I would drive home drunk.

I smoke marijuana which I pick up in New York or San Francisco and start to combine my scotch with "doobies." I find it harder and harder to get or stay high and get angry at my suppliers for selling me lousy crap.

On one foreign trip, Toby and I fly into Paris and drive down to the Loire Valley to visit Sue, a friend who has just bought an old farm house that she plans to refurbish. For several days, I drink some of the best locally-produced French wines at lunch, in the late afternoon, and at dinner.

Because I could speak French, Sue would ask me to talk to local officials about construction issues. In addition, she asked me if I could help her buy a piano for the house. Without any knowledge of the area, Toby and I drove into a town 80 kilometers away, found a piano factory, and convinced the owner to deliver a used up-right piano to Sue's house the day before Christmas. How did I do it? I asked Toby to sing in the store in front of everyone and told them that she was a famous Broadway star.

Every summer Toby and I throw a catered Labor Day party for 50+ guests. Liquor flows constantly and I smoke marijuana in the bathroom or out on our porch overlooking the Great Salt Lake. Life is great when I am drinking, and I feel like I've climbed to the top of the mountain.

At one point, Toby and I run up more than $200,000 in credit card bills and $180,000 in loans against the cash value in our insurance policies. Toby tells me that I am slurring my words, and that I need to slow down my drinking. As usual, I get angry; tell her that she does not know the pressure that I am under, and that great people always drink to get their best ideas.

My insecurity begins to mount, and we argue daily. Often I threaten to leave her and kill myself, and I isolate myself from the rest of the world. My belief in Toby disintegrates to the point that I am angry on a daily basis and begin to drink regularly at 5:00 p.m. Many days I would watch the clock as it slowly ticked towards Happy Hour. While I spiral down to hell, Toby starts to pull away to maintain her own sanity.

I continue to find fault with everyone and everything. One day Toby and I hike with friends Tom and Teresa, and I tell them that I'm God.

Chapter 7
(2002-2003)

ALMOST DEAD
IN NEW YORK CITY

It is now September and we fly to San Francisco for a convention. That evening, I drink too much and yell at Toby in public. She runs off to our hotel room and I go drink some more. The next morning, people come over to tell me they loved my piano playing. Sadly, I do not remember that evening.

In December, we fly to New York to see our friend Kevin. After dinner, Toby heads back to the hotel room while Kevin and I go bar hopping on Second Avenue. While walking back to the hotel, I pass out on Third Avenue and wake up in an emergency room. Everyone is dressed in white, and I think I'm dead. The police report indicates that they found me in my own vomit in a gutter, and that I had been robbed.

Toby awakes in the middle of the night and calls Kevin, who tells her that he left me at an unknown bar. Toby asks the concierge to call the police and hospitals. The concierge tracks me down and Toby and Kevin escort me back to the hotel. We all head down for breakfast as I experience the worst hangover in my life.

The next day we travel to New Jersey to attend a Bas Mitzvah. I get drunk within the first hour, scream at everyone, and tell Toby that she can leave me if she doesn't like what I am doing. Alan, the father of the Bas Mitzvah, tells me in no uncertain terms that I embarrass him and his family. I apologize to Robin, his wife, and break down in front of everyone.

The following month I find out that Mom has added Jill, my sister, to the family master account. For my birthday, I receive a check from Mom, see Jill's name on the joint account, and rip it up. I put both of their names on my Spam list and refuse to answer the phone when they try to reach me.

In March, I tempt fate once again. I lecture in Dublin and fly back to Salt Lake City to spend the weekend with Toby. Unfortunately, she gets called to New York to attend a funeral. Being on my own, I spend the weekend in Las Vegas. That evening, I smoke a couple of J's, go down to the hotel bar, drink, go to the bathroom, and get stopped by hotel security. They tell me that management does not want me there and if I do not leave quietly they will arrest me for trespassing. I argue with the police who immediately handcuff me and cart me off to jail. After spending eight hours in a holding tank with other felons, I am released on my own recognizance.

In April, I attend another conference in Florida. That evening, I race to the bar and order my first double. After many drinks, I stumble around the room slurring my words. Andrew, a business associate, pulls me aside the next morning and tells me that last night's drinks were very expensive. I tell Andrew they were "free." He tells me that it would be cheaper for me to buy my own bottle and drink upstairs in the privacy of my own hotel room. He further adds that

I am losing "potential" clients who do not like my drinking and informs me my glass is a bottomless pit.

Later that day, Steve, another business associate, tells me that he saw me in the lobby the night before, weaving and slurring my words. He adds that I did not recognize him and told him to "piss" off.

It was at that point, that I decided that "enough" was "enough," and I went to the Internet for help. Recognizing that I might have an alcohol problem was not easy. I went feverishly from website to website, rejecting every comment about my drinking behavior. I could not believe that I was an alcoholic since I was neither poor nor lived underneath a bridge.

For weeks, I would wake up wondering if I was an alcoholic. I tried to stop but couldn't and justified every drink I gulped. I rejected any help that my friends offered and thought that I could stop anytime. I wanted to be normal but could not find the means, energy, or will power.

I denied it over and over again. I kept thinking that it could not be happening to me. Then one day, a frightful thought stayed in my mind. Could I really be an alcoholic?

I became obsessed with finding the answer. I spent hours on the Internet reading articles by researchers, doctors, and recovering alcoholics. I searched for every term that I could think of that described my behavior.

To convince myself one way or another, I took an on-line quiz that asked me the following questions. Here are the questions and my answers, as I remember them from that frightful day:

Do you drink at least 4 times a week? YES

Have you had a drink or two at home before you go to

a party where they will serve alcohol? YES

Do you drink the next morning to avoid a hangover? NO

Have you ever had six or more drinks on one occasion? YES

Have you been able to stop drinking after you started? NO

How often have you failed to do what was normally expected from you because of drinking? CANNOT REMEMBER

Have you needed a first drink in the morning to get yourself going after a heavy drinking session? NO

Have you had a feeling of guilt or remorse after drinking? YES

Do you forget what happened the night before because you had been drinking? ALL THE TIME

Have you or someone else been injured as a result of your drinking? YES

Has a relative or friend or a doctor or other health worker been concerned about your drinking or suggested you cut down? YES

In order to stop drinking alcohol have you tried to switch to beer? NO, HATE IT

Have you tried to limit the number of drinks? YES

Do you prefer to drink alone? NO

Have you tried to get rid of the alcohol in your home only to buy some more? NO

Have you stopped drinking during business hours yet think about it? YES

Have you sworn off alcohol forever and started drinking again? YES

Have you talked about exercising more and done
 nothing about it? YES

Have you tried reading inspirational/motivational
 books? YES

Have you attended a health farm recovery program
 and gone back to drinking? NO

Have you mixed alcohol with milk? NEVER

After completing the quiz, I thought I had a drinking
problem. I got angry at the computer and wanted to hammer
it to pieces. My rage was intensive and beyond anything I had
ever experienced before. I began to lie to friends and told
them that I was a borderline alcoholic and that I could still
drink. My drinking problem got worse as I drank up to a 1/3
bottle a day of Glenlivet.

I kept researching alcoholism on the Internet. In March
2003, I finally found the AA website. I downloaded a lot of
material and become overwhelmed by all the AA stories.
For weeks I looked at their site and studied it intensively
while consuming more and more alcohol.

Several paragraphs on the AA website kept drawing me
back:

*"There are many different ideas about what alcoholism
really is. The explanation that seems to make sense is that alcoholism is a progressive illness, which can never be cured but
which can be arrested. Many feel that the illness represents the
combination of a physical sensitivity to alcohol and a mental
obsession with drinking, which, regardless of consequences, cannot be broken by willpower alone."*

*"Once alcoholism has set in, there is nothing morally wrong
about being ill. At this stage, free will is not involved, because the
sufferer has lost the power of choice over alcohol."*

For the first time in my life, I looked at my drink and started to cry. I realized that I was sick and had lost control over my drinking. After checking the online schedule, I decide to go to my first AA meeting.

Chapter 8
(April 2003 – Days 0-30)

WELCOME TO AA

It's Tuesday morning, April 15th, and I'm scared. I drive 10 minutes to a church on the east side of Bountiful. I get there early and anxiously walk around the courtyard. Although I see beautiful flowers all around me, I feel uncomfortable and uneasy. I do not know what to do or say to the people I see milling around.

I walk in the door and accidentally walk into a food pantry. I whisper for directions to the "meeting" and they point me to the back entrance. Before I leave, they ask me to move my car off the street since the neighbors do not like to see their parking spaces tied up by a bunch of "drunks." As I walk back to my car, I feel small and ashamed.

After moving my car to the parking lot, I reenter the church from the rear. I see an older gentleman in the hallway and ask him about the "meeting." He smiles and tells me to come with him. He accompanies me down the stairs to a room which is filled with "donated" furniture from the 1950s.

As we await the "meeting," he tells me his name is Bill and asks if I would like some freshly brewed coffee. I nod yes. Several other people slowly enter the room. They seem to know each other and chat up a storm.

The meeting begins, and they ask if there any "newcomers" who are there for their "first" or "second" meeting.

I raise my hand and say "I'm Jeffrey." They smile and say "Welcome."

The meeting, which reminds me of a ritual, continues. Since the meeting is small, everyone gets to talk or pass. I listen to people talk openly and honestly about their alcoholic experiences. Many talk about their "near death" experiences and relate "horrible" stories about their friends who died from alcohol abuse. They all tell me that "newcomers" are special, and that I should attend 90 meetings in 90 days.

Many people at the meeting quote the "Big Book" (written in 1939 by Bill W., one of the founders of Alcoholics Anonymous), and they show me a copy. Everyone tells me to buy it and read it. I said "What should I do after I read it?" They smile and repeat in unison, "Read it again!" I pull out my wallet and give them a $5 bill.

During the first week, I attend three meetings and listen to people share their problems. I learn very quickly that alcoholics cannot control their drinking, that the disease is progressive, and that there is no cure. The only solution is to not take the first drink.

Without liquor in my diet, I turn to coffee, soda and "sweet" things to quench my craving for sugar. My recovering buddies tell me to eat lots of hard candy and watch out for warning signs such as being hungry, angry, lonely, or tired (HALT). They tell me that when I feel HALT, to get to a meeting.

Daily, I get upset with what I hear. At the end of every meeting, they tell me to "keep coming back" and encourage me to find a "sponsor" who can help guide me through my recovery. After four days I ask Bill to be my sponsor and he accepts. For the first month, I attend at least one meeting a day and sometimes go to two, three or four in a row. I share with my newfound friends my anger and my need to get "cured."

I notice quickly that no one answers my questions. They all nod and tell me to read the "Big Book" which angers me more. I question everything I hear and read. I analyze the meetings and tell myself that I am not an alcoholic and they are not like me.

I hear a lot of new words and phrases like "normie" (a person who drinks like a normal human being), "pink cloud" (a false feeling that everything is wonderful), "camel chip" (a plastic coin that represents an animal that can go for days without drinking), "going out" (a person who starts drinking again), and "relapse" (a person who returns to meetings after "going out.")

After a couple of weeks, I am sick of listening to people's stories and continue to tell mine. No one seems to care and they accuse me of being selfish. I question why I take this abuse from total strangers and constantly think that I do not belong there. But I realize that I cannot stop drinking and that I've run out of alternatives.

During the second week, while I am getting my hair cut, Cindy stares at my bald spots and tells me I am starting to grow hair again. She asks me if I am using treatments, and I tell her that I'm in an alcoholic recovery program.

On my 14th day, Toby and I go to an MS fundraiser at Snowbird. I sit with John, who has MS, and does not drink. I watch everyone in the room and see that they are having a lot of fun. I tell people that I'm in an alcoholic recovery program and that I can never drink again. Since they are all "buzzed" they do not hear me. I see them slur their words, trip as they walk, and float from table to table. My anger grows as I see myself in their faces.

After an hour, I tell Toby that I can't take it. I get up, say goodbye to the host, and tell my wife that I'll wait for her outside in the car. She quickly gets up and tells me that she'll come with me since she does not want me to be alone.

On my 16th day, I attend a conference in Dallas. I get the Dallas AA meeting schedule, skip lunch, and go to a meeting. As I arrive, I see lots of trucks, enter the "meeting hall," and learn that liquor does not care whether you are from "Yale" or "jail."

On my 18th day, I begin to write my 30-day speech. I have this brilliant idea to write a 5-minute essay on the value of the program using only words from the "Big Book." I tell my idea to Kit who shares with me that his son is a recovering alcoholic and, as a gift, sends me the electronic version of the "Big Book."

I share my plan at meetings and people scoff, telling me that it is a theatrical act to get attention. I deny everything and proceed to write and rewrite my speech at 3:00 in the morning when I cannot sleep.

On my 30th day, I wake up excited to share my new-found wisdom. At the noon meeting, I confidently raise my hand, walk to the front of the room, accept my 30-day chip, and share the following:

Attention Drunks. Willing to learn? Sit, rest, relax, and listen.

Alcoholism is a disease and an illness. Its insanity has prevented me from finding my Higher Power, good coffee, intoxicating chocolate and a New York delicatessen here in Utopia.

Am I ugly, unapproachable, uncommunicative, unfa-
vorable, unimportant, unmanageable, unpopular,
unusual, unwelcome?
I am not unique.
There are many men, women, children, brothers,
husbands, wives, and mothers who think just like
me. There are many who are sick, tired, cold and
frightened of this unfair, unjust world just like me.
I am not unique.
Can I be helped? Abandon my past?
Wine, absurd, whiskey, stupid, drugs, ridiculous,
alcohol, devastating.
Yes. It's simple. Just stop drinking. 24 Hours a day. Is
it possible? Yes. Just look around the room. When will
I, the alcoholic, get cured? Sorry, never. Yet, there is a
solution. And it works.
Bear witness to a new-found concept: Twelve Steps,
Twelve Principles.
Go tell your personal story to a group of anonymous
drinkers. Talk without limitation and undergo
change. There are no critics here. Problems, troubles,
vicissitudes? Just ask. Cannot? Ashamed, embar-
rassed? Get over it. Get with the program. No need to
do it alone.
Feel sad? Laugh. Keep coming back. Dislike job?
Leave. Miserable circumstances? Remove yourself.
Hate employer? Quit.
Always another chance, another opportunity on the
horizon.
Why here? Why this particular organization?
It's the fellowship and love. It's the peace of sobriety.

*No more hangover, body abuse, potential painful
death. Doubt this? The Big Book clearly explains.
People die from drinking.*

Want help? First, lose your attitude.

*Come to meetings, Saturday, Sunday, Tuesday,
everyday, mornings, afternoons, evenings.
Listen with an open mind, learn from others'
experiences. Read the big book daily and treat
yourself with respect.*

*Will you find words in the big book that you don't
understand? Sure. Here are a few. Bedevilments.
Belladonna. Delirium. Doggerel. Elba. Gaunt.
Maelstrom. Nadir. Pandemonium. Prosaic.
Remonstrances. Tremens.*

*Will you find dirty words in the book? Yes. Here are a
few. Lips kissed. Roused. Bathtub. Sex. Bondage.
Lubricant. Self-propulsion. Thunderbolts. Swallowed.
Satisfaction.*

*Our creator, who forgives and accepts, in his vast,
absolute, wonder has wonderful wishes and guidance
for you and me. We must discover and continually
rediscover the answers to a fulfilling life.*

*Do not judge. Let someone else do the driving for a
change.*

*I must learn to be patient. I know that I will see signs
on my journey. I just do not know where I am going.
I have the rest of my life to work on it. The book says
it. I believe it. I am convinced. Faith works. It is
absolute and beautiful.*

*Before AA I failed. I tried every method known to
man.*

Spiritual miracles do happen and I wanted to share my new-found happiness with you today. If I can do it, so can you. No more alibis, excuses. May God bless everybody, everything, everywhere forever. With 30 days sober, I'll take another 24.

Chapter 9
(May 2003 – Days 30-60)

DEALING WITH ANGER

With 30 days sober, I lose track of time. Frequently, I worry that my marriage may fail. I find some relief in my daily alcoholic recovery meetings, but I feel lonely and depressed.

I miss alcohol and have crazy dreams at night. I remember good times, but I awake suddenly at 2 or 3 in the morning on a regular basis and go on the Internet for solace.

Bill, my sponsor, tells me that I cannot survive on meetings alone and tells me that I need to start working the 12 steps outlined in the "Big Book." He encourages me to start Step 1 which requires me to admit that alcohol is too powerful for me and that my life is unmanageable.

I reluctantly begin. At this point, I have nothing to lose. Bill hands me an 11- page document to read on anger and a form to fill out which requires me to think about my past and delve into my anger. I tell him that I've had 10 years of group and individual therapy, and that I do not need his help. I remind Bill how smart I am and try to pummel him into the ground.

I asked Bill "What does anger have to do with my wanting to stop drinking?" He laughs and tells me to read the pages and then get back to him. After I read the pages, a light bulb goes off in my head:

- Not accepting the world results in anger
- Many of us express anger much more easily than tenderness
- When we are on our own, we are at our worst
- Anger may have been more acceptable in our families than fear or grief
- Some angers can't be resolved; some partnerships dissolve when they yield more rage than pleasure
- Sometimes we cannot punish the person we are angry with so we take it out on an innocent bystander
- Anger driven inward results in some destructive form
- I cannot punish anyone without punishing myself
- Taking responsibility for my anger, by admitting it, is the first step toward a return to sanity and balance

In spite of my intellectually understanding Bill, I fault him for his tiny flaws; seeing his vain attempts to control me. After a couple of weeks, I dismiss him and leave his forms on a meeting chair for him to discover.

Not in touch with my immaturity, I run around the Club telling everyone how I have been mistreated by my sponsor. All of them tell me to stop whining, grow up, and apologize to Bill. I respond with more anger, attend other meetings in town, and start all over again with fresh faces.

Days pass by and my resentments with Toby, Bill, other Club members, life in general, and my dwindling bank account grow geometrically. I get angry at everything, including the weather. I think about alcohol constantly and fantasize about having a small drink. Club members remind me of my alcoholic binges, my unhappiness during my drinking years, and that "This too shall pass." I shrug off their clichés and hold onto my anger, fearing to let go.

I go through two other sponsors, finding fault with both of them. I think often about killing myself but know in my heart I do not have the guts to do it. I fantasize about my death and how sorry everyone will be without me.

At one point I'm going to four meetings a day. I talk more than I should and hardly listen. I continue to pontificate that I am unique, should not be there, have great plans for my own recovery, and that I do not need them.

Toby cries a lot and does not know how to help me. I feel totally lost and question life as I know it.

One day I get a phone call from a guy I just met named Troy. He tells me he is at the Club and tells me that he is scared. I remember having given him my card but never thought he would call. I hear panic in his voice.

I immediately tell Toby that I need to get down to the Club. I enter the Club and tell Troy to join me in the car. We drive around for 30 minutes. Troy is very hesitant to talk to me and admits that he is afraid of talking to me for fear that he may be doing something wrong.

I listen to him, tell him that I am his friend, and drop him back off at the Club. I have only seen him once since then at another meeting.

As the weeks go by, I argue with Toby on a daily basis. I tell her that I'm an alcoholic and refer her to the "Big Book." She is totally lost and does not believe a word that I am saying. I encourage her to come to a meeting with me. She continues to reject the concept that she needs help as well.

One day I run into Bill, my first sponsor, and apologize. I do not know exactly why I did it, but I felt bad for mistreating him and did not want to interfere with my progress.

My friends tell me that carrying resentments triggers drinking and that I did the right thing.

Toby and I vacation in New York, and I elect to attend a meeting at AA headquarters. I believe it is at this point that I begin my transformation. I was sitting in the meeting overlooking the Hudson River and there was no denying the spirit in that room. I walked around and saw hundreds of memorabilia of Bill W and Dr. Bob, the founders of AA. The experience was magical and mystical.

The next day I attend a meeting at the 79th Street Workshop which runs 110 meetings a week. Having grown up Jewish, it seemed weird to attend a meeting in a basement church with lots of strangers. The irony is that as soon as I walked into the room, I felt safe and at home.

In the remaining few days before receiving my 60-day chip, I chaired several meetings, met many newcomers, prepared coffee, and listened. I found listening to be the hardest thing to do. Many times I was annoyed at how people presented their problems and thought that their problems were so insignificant compared to mine. Looking back, I have to laugh at my own arrogance.

Slowly I begin to listen to other people's problems. My new interim sponsor tells me that it's OK to help others as long as it does not interfere with my own recovery. Throughout a two-week period, I learn about people who were dying of cancer, had died sober, had died alone and drunk, had lost their homes, jobs, wives, and families, had gone to or just came out of jail, relapsed, gone back to drugs, returned for another try, lost their driving privileges, lost their licenses, and had their children taken away.

I learned about an older woman who had asked me to

chair a meeting. A week later I returned to the same meeting and did not see her. Another week passed. I then saw the
woman and thanked her for letting me chair the meeting
two weeks prior. I asked her where she had been . She told
me that she could only come to a meeting when she had
extra cash because she was living on a $1 a day and the bus
fare was $1.60. After hearing those age-worn words, I went
out to my car and wept.

On June 12, two days before I am to receive my 60-day
chip, I receive the following e-mail from a person who calls
himself Stonecoldcreed:

**You need to go back over the 12 traditions of
A.A. You have broken at least 8 of them on
your sorry website. Not to mention you even
gave out someones name. Only 30 days sober
and you are already a pro and know everything
there is to know about the aa program. You are
a true example of some on who thinks they are
to smart for this program and you are going to
fail. Not to mention the people you will infect
and what about the new comers. You have nothing to offer people at all. You, your book and
your website are worth less than a few sheets
of charmin. Get with the program or get drunk!
You really need to check yourself before you
spread our illness to others and not show recovery. I'll be in touch to check up on how you will
be doing. No, that is not a threat. It is one
Alcoholic looking after another. Besides, I
might know you!**

Good Luck,
STONECOLD

I immediately freak and think that a crazy person is out to get me. I calm myself down and write this response.

STONECOLD,
Thanks for your opinion. I know this may be hard for you to believe but I believe that I am doing the right thing. Unless I am mistaken, I have not divulged anyone's full name, address, telephone number and thus preserved their anonymity. I list my contact information because the law requires me to do so.
I have also not listed myself as a A.A. member. I have quoted the "Big Book" and only alcoholics would know that.
If I have helped at least one other person, without harming others, than I have done God's will. And in the short-time that my websites have been up 6 people have told me to continue with my good work. So far, you are outnumbered.
As a writer and author, I have always been surrounded by critics. I have always believed that when God created authors, writers, actors, directors, musicians and the like, He used the finest Marble that He could create. And with the chips, that were left over, He made critics. If you are so sure of yourself, than you would not hide behind a moniker.

Oh, by the way, I get my 60-day chip on Saturday and I'm doing fine. Thanks for asking.

He and I corresponded for 3 days. On the first day, I received one e-mail, two on the second, and eight on the third. When I mentioned this incident to members at the Club, the e-mails stopped.

On advice from Don, my 4th sponsor, I did not write a 60-day speech. Instead, I talked from the heart. It was Sunday, June 16th, Father's Day, and Toby was in New York with her family. As I started to talk about changes in my life I cried in front of the 50-75 people at the meeting.

Chapter 10
(June 2003 – Days 60-90)

HAVE YOU MET DON,
MY SPONSOR?

It is now June 2003. I have just received my 60-day chip and plot my strategy to get a 90-day chip. Slowly but surely I start to think more about others and less about myself. Unfortunately, I relapse a lot into my former angry self, which now appears more randomly with a sharper, vicious tongue.

Toby gets more upset and tells me that she does not need my advice. She reluctantly goes to an Al-Anon meeting and runs into Bill, my former sponsor. Later that evening, she tells me that she did not like the meeting and thought that everyone was a whiner.

My daily routine evolves. Now I work in the morning and attend a 12:00 meeting on a daily basis. Often, I throw in an extra meeting on Wednesday and attend morning meetings on Saturday and Sunday. After 73 days of sobriety, I have gone to 90 meetings as suggested.

I read the "Big Book" at night, begin to recognize phrases as members share their experiences, and quote the "Big Book" at meetings. My transition feels natural and others begin to see a new me.

In order to start each day calmly, I sit outside on the

porch with my first cup of coffee. One day I share with Toby my need for a hummingbird feeder. Toby reluctantly agrees since back East we had a regular bird feeder and watched birds shit all over their food.

Great moments are interspersed with horrible fights. Toby's son, daughter-in-law, and two grandkids come out to visit and I get angry at the slightest disturbances, like the grandkids talking during TV programs, messing up the kitchen, using the treadmill unsupervised, and wanting to climb the Jungle Jim at McDonalds for the 17th time. I typically react by taking my anger into the car and driving over to the Club for serenity.

Interwoven with tense moments are memories that will last a lifetime, including teaching both the 5-and 7-year olds to play chopsticks on the piano, baking a pie with cherries that they handpicked from our garden, going to a movie, eating Skiddles, watching the Macy's 4th of July fireworks on TV while having a picnic in our TV room, and eating steak and fresh corn on the patio while watching the evening sun slowly fade into the Western sky over the Great Salt Lake.

Don, my new sponsor, meets with me for coffee to discuss my progress. He and I agree that I feel fairly comfortable with the first few steps. Step 3 is tough because it requires me to acknowledge that a Higher Power exists and that only He can help me solve my problem. Don tells me that I need to define my own Higher Power and that, if I feel uncomfortable with God, I can substitute the group, a tree, or anything else I want as long as it is not me.

In spite of the fact that I am not doing well on my own, I am deathly afraid to turn my life over to another person, let alone God. Don tells me that I do not need to turn my life over but only to acknowledge that I am willing to begin and give it a try. He calms me down and reassures me. For the first time, I feel that I am in good hands and on the right track.

Don continues to monitor my progress everyday. At this point, I take out a full-time Club membership. I begin to sit on the Club porch with others before and after the meeting. I begin to feel like I am with family and that everyone is there for each other. For service work, I chair meetings, donate pies, and greet newcomers.

Unfortunately, as I spend more time at the Club, I redis-cover cigarettes. I ask several people for advice. They all tell me that if it will help my sobriety, it's OK. I also learn that I can eat chocolate, hard candies, and French fries – any-thing to stop the desire for alcohol.

I find that staying sober saps my energy. There are days that I get so depressed that I cannot even work. At one point, my e-mail inbox had over 1,000 messages in it. Daily, I talk to my sponsor who reminds me that it is my responsibility to make decisions, not him or Toby, and that I need to get balance in my life.

On June 24th, Don hands me a form, says to copy it, and fill it in each night before I go to bed. In column one are attributes called personality characteristics of self-will and in the second column are attributes called personality char-acteristics of God's-Will.

On the first night, I pull out the form which tells me to review my day and check off whether I demonstrated char-acteristics of self-will or God's-will. There are 22 attributes in each column. On the first night, I checked off 9 which indicated my self-will:

- Pride
- Lustful
- Anger
- Gluttony
- Impatient
- Resentment
- Self-Justification
- Self-Importance
- Suspicion

For five nights, I complete the forms and then stop since I do not see the value of performing this ritual. On the business front, revenue is dropping quickly.

Toby and I attend another MS fundraiser, and I share with people that I'm in an alcoholic recovery program. To my surprise, people seem interested and know others who have battled alcoholism. I slowly begin to realize the extent that this disease has affected everyone around me.

After 80 days in my recovery, I feel reinvented and wonderful. At this point, I talk to God often. It now seems natural to ask Him for guidance.

On my 86th day, I awake at 4:11 a.m. and feel God asking me to walk with Him throughout the house. Without missing a beat, I jump out of bed and feel His presence. After touring upstairs, we descend downstairs . I see a picture on the wall and look at it for several minutes. I'm in the center of the picture, drinking with my "friends" at a party. God asks me if I'm having fun. I say "yes." He then asks me if I missed it. I say "yes." I then ask him, "Was it that bad?" He says, "What do you think?" I smile and say, "They were my drinking buddies. I do not socialize with any of them now. I have nothing in common with them."

Chapter 11
(July 2003 – October 2003 – Months 3-6)

WHATEVER IT TAKES

I underestimated how hard it would be to stay in the moment for the last 90 days. I originally thought that if I could make it through 30 days, I could make it through 90 days with the same level of effort. I was wrong.

On three separate occasions I watch "My Name is Bill W.", which depicts the life story of the two AA co-founders. Every time I watch the movie, I see myself portrayed in James Woods' character.

I read a lot of recovery books, including the "AA Big Book", "12 and 12", "Living Sober", and "Daily Reflections for Recovering People" and frequently quote passages at meetings.

Even though recovery is hard, life in general is good. But anger raises its ugly head every time I see others with a drink in their hand. Frequently, I walk out on social events where they serve alcohol, and I begin to see things that Toby does not see. At one event I see dancing glasses and cannot get the nightmarish vision out of my mind. David, a doctor friend from California, tries to calm me down as I rush down the street to my car, a safe place. He even goes as far as to tell me that he has been in recovery. But, I do not believe him because he cannot produce his sobriety chip.

At home, things are bad. New York friends come out to

visit their son in a wilderness program and have wine on our back porch while I wince in silence. Toby's son and family come out to visit and I avoid them. To get through these tough times, I hang out at meetings with my recovering friends and withdraw completely from alcohol-laden social events.

Toby and I perform at our first sober wedding. It feels strange to set up my keyboard and not be able to smoke a reefer or drink a couple of scotches before our performance. I am more cognizant of the audience this time and have difficulty accepting their applause.

I fly to Los Angeles to meet a man who wants me to go to Sri Lanka to lecture on equipment leasing. I enjoy his company and have a diet Coke while he drinks some hot tea. The experience seems surrealistic because I am very cognizant of the conversation. For the first time, I ask God to bless this man in his travels and hug him before he gets into a cab to the airport.

Back at the Club, my sponsor and I are getting along real well. I am on Step 4 which requires me to write down my resentments, fears and harms. It takes me 6 weeks to complete the process and I feel inadequate. People come over to me and point out my progress. I ask them how long it took them to complete Step 4 and many said years.

Toby runs into the Club hysterical, after we have a major fight. I had told her that many marriages break apart when one gets sober since the equilibrium in the relationship changes.

Don, my sponsor, sees her running after me in the Club and tells her to sit down and read the "Big Book" and suggests that she go to an Al-Anon meeting. For the next several weeks, she and I start to talk recovery and I feel lucky to have a wife concerned about my disease.

Going to meetings, reading the "Big Book", praying to God, working with a sponsor, and helping others become more and more of my daily routine. But, it is not enough. So, I create a website dedicated to recovery, start an Internet newsletter, and respond on-line to people all over the world who seek help.

Although I like most of the people at the Club, I still have fights and disagreements, walk out on some meetings, and complain to others. Most people laugh at me and tell me to get over it. They tell me that I am taking other people's inventory (Step 4) and that I allow these people to rent space in my brain for free.

On the business front, my consulting projects dwindle and we have to dip into our savings to supplement our irregular cash flow. Slowly but surely, my business solidifies as I become more comfortable with economic insecurity.

Toby and I head over to Amsterdam on vacation. In the evenings we go to AA meetings. I like the international format and instead of passing the basket for donations, they pass a wooden shoe.

On the way back from Amsterdam, we stop in New York to visit family. Again, I cannot handle the stress, and skip Toby's son's surprise 40th birthday party. Instead, I meet a friend who accompanies me to an AA meeting. While heading over, he introduces me to a great recovery shop in Manhattan called Choices , where I buy books, stickers, desk items and inspirational posters.

More New York friends come out to visit. They tell me how great I look and that I seem to be calmer. I politely accept their compliment and slowly realize that everyone else sees changes that I do not.

One week I am in New York, Chicago, and San Francisco on business. At the end of the day I attend AA meetings. I am impressed that anyone can go anywhere in the world and find an AA meeting.

Toby and I go to our first Club picnic. I feel weird because I would never have socialized with these people before. The old Jeffrey would have found many prejudicial and stupid reasons to not hang out with them. As time progresses I become more aware of my own stupidity. But, I am unable to forgive myself.

Toby and I head off to Hawaii and I go to a 12 Coconuts meeting on the beach. Stupidly, I sit on the ground, while others sit in their fold-out chairs. I look down and see ants crawling all over my legs.

I continue to travel, lecture during the day, and attend meetings at night. Some days I fall asleep and miss both meetings and dinner.

In late September, Mickey B. flies in from California to speak at our Saturday night speaker meeting. The room is packed with 200 sober people and all of us crack up at his drunk/sober jokes. For the first time, I am proud to be a recovering alcoholic.

Back at the Club, Margaret, who chairs the Club Board, drives me crazy because she thinks she knows it all. I ask people about her and many say that she does not go to daily meetings and has lost touch with the rest of us. Suddenly, her husband dies and I see her differently. Now we hug each other and barb amicably.

During the final weeks of this recovery phase, I tell the

Club members that I dropped a bar of soap down the toilet and can't flush without it overflowing. They suggest that I buy a plunger, pour liquid plumber down the toilet, augur it, or use another toilet and stop complaining. For some reason, I cannot get the toilet to stop overflowing and wait patiently for two weeks before the soap self-dissolves.

Socially, I regress to when I was 10 years old. I feel like a wall flower at outside social events and find that I have nothing to talk about except my recovery.

One week before I receive my 6-month chip, Toby goes back into the hospital for her third back surgery. The first one, ten years prior, fused her lower back. The doctors removed her steel rod in the second surgery. This procedure created more space at the top of Toby's back so that her bones and ligaments would not touch her nerves, which had been sending shooting pains down her back and legs.

I am on the road and miss Toby's surgery which is now postponed due to her coming down with asthmatic bronchitis. To deal with my emotional pain, I eat muffins and/or Danish for breakfast, brownies before lunch, cookies in the afternoon, Atkins Bars at the hotel, and Death by Chocolate for dessert.

As much as I love Toby, I cannot stand her as a patient. She complains about everything, especially when I misunderstand her orders. Her back pain worsens as the pain meds no longer work. She screams throughout the night and my fears come true —Toby may be addicted to narcotics.

I run to the Club the next day, pour out my soul, cry aimlessly, go to a meeting, get my 6-month chip, get yelled at by my sponsor for getting the chip a day early, reluctantly give back the chip, go home to deal with Toby, return to the

Club the next day, get my chip, and head off to Los Angeles.

I call Toby that night and talk to an AA friend who has agreed to baby sit her. I end our conversation, hang up the phone, and fall exhausted on my hotel bed. Before I retire I read the "Big Book" and think about all of the people that I need to make amends to. And there are many.

Chapter 12
(October 2003 – January 2004 – Months 6-9)

I COULD NOT DO IT ALONE

For the last three months I have taken numerous turns in my brain's roller coaster, Ferris wheel, and Tilt-A-Whirl. I circle endlessly like a child, throw up, and go on one more time, seeking pleasure that never comes.

Toby completes her 3rd major surgery and is in constant pain. She takes meds every 4 hours and has so many narcotics in her body that I worry about her potential addiction. When I talk about her at meetings, addicts come over to me, share their experiences, and offer to help me out at home.

There are times that Toby cannot control going to the bathroom and seems infantile as she runs to the bathroom and misses the bowl. Not knowing what to do, I run around the house spraying Lysol. In a way, that was how my alcoholic life was before I started to go to meetings. Instead of dealing with the problem and correcting the underlying issues, I sprayed myself with Lysol and pretended to smell good.

Toby wakes in the middle of the night screaming. She calls on the walkie talkie (which I keep downstairs so that I can hear her when I work late at night) asking me for help. One time, the battery goes dead and I hear her through the walls. Another time, she stumbles in the hallway and almost cripples herself.

During the day, I go over to the Club. One night the Club raises $150 to buy a karaoke machine for the Halloween party after realizing that they were spending a lot of money renting it each year. Considering how broke alcoholics are, we raised the money in less than 5 minutes.

For several weeks, I travel on business and miss a lot of Toby's recovery from back surgery. Friends come to visit and take care of her. After two weeks, Toby is up and running (the doctor told her to rest for six to eight weeks).

After six months in the program, I begin to share about my past and I cry often. My sponsor suggests that I should not share for 30 days and, instead, listen to other's stories. He suggests that I need to get out of myself and see that I am not much different than others. I fight him every step of the way, citing my unique upbringing. In my mind, I hear his words as commands and that if I do not do what he suggests, I will fail.

One day, I receive the following e-mail:

"dear jeffery, give up the cross you seem to think people pick on you. the truth is their is a lot of people that respect you even me. so quit feeling sorry for your self. so like i said give up the cross we need the wood."

To get even, I sent the following response and cc'd everyone in the Club's mailing list:

"Before I respond, I want you to know that I have cc'd all known members of the Club (plus

a few friends that I trust) to make sure that everyone is aware of my decision to not share or chair for 30 days at the Club. This was precipitated by several senior sobers, including my sponsor, who suggested that I do not talk because I could use a maturing experience. Although I disagree with their logic, I will go along with their suggestion. This does not mean that I am happy with my decision."

"In order to tackle this difficult assignment, I have elected to remain silent before, during and after meetings. I have also elected to take notes and will share them with other sobers that I trust. Because, frankly, I do not trust most of the people at the club right now."

"So, here is my response?"

"Who the fuck do you think you are telling me how I should feel? Your insensitivity to my being a Jew using Christian references does not surprise me. The fact that your e-mail name is not on the Club contact list does not surprise me. I have put your name on my SPAM list."

"Oh, if you think you're smarter or wiser than me because you may have more sobriety, you are badly mistaken."

After receiving a copy of the original e-mail and my response, many members reminded me that there are people out there sicker than me and that I should pray for them. In addition, they told me that I was breaking up Club unity and violating the principle of helping the common good.

With that advice I got angrier and would not talk to people for days. I would walk into meetings and walk past people without saying hello. Within a short 24 hours I tried to piss off more than two dozen people. The irony is that no one got angry – not one single person. The only person I hurt was me.

My sponsor e-mailed me with his viewpoints:

"What control do you have over those people? Who cares what they think. You treat them as you would any other sick person. This is not about you. There are several young people in the club that look up to you. They are hurt by your avoidance of them, you are avoiding hugs, handshakes, etc. We think selfishness and self-centerness is the root of our problem. Go ahead and share. We go to any length to stay sober. The most important person in the room is the newcomer. We try to be an example to the newcomer. What are your actions conveying to them? Review your motives and act accordingly. Don't shut down your lifeline to recovery."

I slowly began to realize that an alcoholic loves to be the focus of attention. For most of my life, I loved being on stage, writing and carrying out my script. That is why suicide appealed to me. In my brain, I would have the audience come to attention and applaud with fervor. At times, I thought about writing my own funeral and videotaping it. I even planned out what people would eat at my funeral, as if I could participate in the "timely" event.

On Wednesday, October 29th I went to five meetings —
10:00, 12:00, 5:15, 7:00, and 8:30 and promised to make Toby
dinner. First, I called her to postpone dinner and then can-
celed it. After a day of marathon meetings, I realized that I
was holding on to my anger.

I complained to Don that I needed to share and that
people were laughing at me. So, he wrote me the following:

**"Not speaking in the meeting is only a sugges-
tion. Day one did for you, the same thing it
did for me. I got a resentment I had to work on.
Everyone is making a joke out of it right now,
but as time goes on they will respect you for it.
I don't know if many of those "senior sobers"
could or would go 30 days without speaking.
Sharing after the meeting is part of the process.
After a few days you'll be able to hear. Things
like, who talks recovery, what step a person is
on, who has or has not done the steps, who has
something you want, and more importantly
who has nothing you want. So go forward with
love and tolerance, and remember resentment
is the #1 offender for alcoholics."**

So, on Saturday, November 1, I went to a speaker meeting and listened to 4 people who had less than 1 year sobriety. I listened intently and smiled because I could relate to
their stories. For the first time, I smiled and Brent told me
that I had a spiritual awakening as a result of listening and
not feeling the need to talk. That was the day I began to listen more and talk less.

Once I started to listen and keep my mouth shut, a lot of great things started to happen. Although I was still scared and frightened about my future, I felt pretty good about myself and my prospects for a serene life. As I started to calm down and listen, members started to tell me what a nice person I was.

One of the members, Brent, introduced me to his wife, Jennifer. For a week or so, I would watch Brent and Jennifer hold hands in a meeting. I admired them for sharing their recovery with the group and still remember the day when Brent told me that he was Don's sponsor.

Then I found out that Mel, a cowboy alcoholic, was Brent's sponsor. I could not believe that I had a sponsor, grand sponsor and great grand sponsor all at the same Club. That night, I thanked God for my good fortune.

One day, Brent invites me, along with a dozen other alcoholics, to his house to share his 15th AA Birthday. Michelle and I run to the grocery store to get ice cream for the group. Running up and down the aisles, we throw containers of ice cream, fudge, whipped cream, sprinkles, and nuts into the wobbly cart. Eating ice cream with my friends, listening to their stories, and sitting on the floor by the fireplace made me feel like Sandra Bullock in "While You Were Sleeping."

Don keeps me reading the "Big Book", which I study and practice. Periodically, I would read and re-read certain passages, including some of the personal stories at the back of the book. One of my favorite and inspirational stories, Bondage, talks about a lady who focuses on money and material wealth. And, just as she, I learned that after I stopped focusing on money, I began to feel happy.

In late November, Toby is still recovering from back surgery and I want to take her to Rome to meet up with Jordana, my oldest daughter, who is studying in Athens. We spend 6 days in Rome touring the Coliseum, Forum, Borghese Park, Republic Square, and the Vatican. The weather is delightful yet on the chilly side. We eat croissants and jelly for breakfast, dine on pizza for lunch, pig out on pasta for dinner and finish the day with gelato and pastries. God does have a strange sense of humor. On the last day, my body reacts to the carbo loading and I want a drink so badly that I see dancing bottles. I begin to withdraw and exhibit my old feelings. I start to mope, feel sorry for myself, and drown in self-pity.

When we get back from Rome, I go to 5 meetings the very next day. I learn that alcoholics can react to too much bread, pasta, pizza, ice cream, cake, and cookies because it triggers the desire for alcohol. Phil, a Club member, says it brilliantly – "An alcoholic brain will lie to you in order to kill you."

Just before Thanksgiving I complete my 9th step, which is very difficult since I had to share my alcoholic past with my family and enemies. I feel humiliated and do not want to share this personal discovery with anyone who I think can still hurt me. My sponsor tells me that I have to let go in order to recover and that "This too shall pass." It was tough telling people that I was sorry for what I had done and offer my amends.

At this time of the year, my training business slows down and cash flow drops to a minimum. My websites and book sales bring in a little money. I talk to a lot of prospects and hear the same line, "Let's talk after the Holidays." In order to pay bills on time, I ask Toby to liquidate some of her retirement assets since I do not want to go to my family for money.

Just before I leave for my next international trip, my sister, Jill, and my Mom give me part of my inheritance to help pay off my substantial credit card debt. They say that they are pleased with my progress and hope that I can start afresh. At that point, I fall to my knees and thank God.

Toby and I cancel Thanksgiving when we find out that Toby's 5-year-old granddaughter, Paige, has developed diabetes. We learn that she will have to take a daily injection of insulin the rest of her life. I pray to God for guidance and make every effort to not get angry.

I continue to watch movies about alcoholism, rate them 1 to 5 stars, put my reviews on my website, and lend them to my friends at the Club.

On Saturday, November 29, I leave Salt Lake City and 21 hours later arrive in Colombo, Sri Lanka. There are only two flights a day from London to Sri Lanka and the early one is sold out. So, I sit in Heathrow for 12 hours. I walk up and down Terminal 4 at least a dozen times, visit the smoking area at least 6 times, walk into every department store at least twice, drink 6 cups of coffee and wash it down with anything that has chocolate in it.

Walking by the bars is tempting but I did not drink.

Boarding the flight to Sri Lanka takes forever. There are 4 crying babies within 5 feet of my ears. When one stops crying, another one starts. As a result of this non-stop assault to the senses, and the incredibly small, declining-challenged seat, I cannot sleep. To make matters worse, my in-seat screen does not work and they cannot move me. To keep my sanity, I read a book, which I picked up in Heathrow, called *Armed and Dangerous, Straight Answers from The Bible.*

Here are some quotes which I found interesting:

- "Thou shall not kill"
- "Do not be deceived…drunkards will not inherit the Kingdom of God"
- "A fool gives full vent to his anger…"
- "For we brought nothing into this world, and it is certain we can carry nothing out"
- "Live in harmony with one another"
- "To every thing there is a season, and a time to every purpose under the heaven…"

Finally, I arrive at Colombo's Bandaranaike International Airport, situated near the town of Katunayake, 20 miles north of Colombo. To Sri Lankans, their island is the original Garden of Eden. Unfortunately, much forestry was burned by the British, who wanted to plant coffee and tea. But there are still substantial tracts of scrub jungle and rainforests. The west and south coasts of Sri Lanka are uniformly low and fringed with coconut trees.

My driver picks me up and takes me to the hotel in downtown Colombo. There is only one road and it is filled with small three wheelers, bicycles, motorcycles, over-crowded buses, and an occasional large car weaving its way by tiny stores, where the owners tout their wares to locals trudging through mud-packed, make-shift sidewalks.

After several days lecturing, my client takes me to a local Sri Lankan restaurant at the Hilton. Prior to dinner we play some pool and listen to American music in the British-like pub. Under the careful guidance of my host, I am intro-duced to all types of local fare. I remember watching the swaying palm trees, sipping my non-alcoholic beverages and enjoying paradise.

After a quick ride to the airport at midnight, I board my plane to London. Sure enough, I sit next to more crying babies, try to smile, take a sleeping pill, and pray to God that I will make it to London without screaming, yelling, or pulling a trigger.

Upon arrival in London, I find out that all flights to New York are cancelled due to severe snow storms on the East Coast. My instincts tell me that I better book another flight the next day and find a hotel for the evening.

British Airways estimates that 60,000 passengers had been stranded in London. With United Airlines adding another 140,000 to the stranded list, I knew I was in deep trouble. I still remember the exhausted people at British Airways laughing at me when I asked them to find my luggage.

After booking a room at the Comfort Inn, I wait outside at the airport bus depot for an hour. I am freezing and do not have my winter coat with me, since I had conveniently packed it in my New York-bound luggage. The trip to the hotel took 40 minutes and I stayed in my room all night without ever leaving for dinner.

I wake up at 5:00 a.m. and take the first bus back to Heathrow. My 8:30 flight leaves on time. Although there are no crying babies, the in-flight entertainment system is down. When I get to New York, British Airways tells me that they lost my luggage.

At this point, I have been in the same clothes for 36 hours. In order to get over to Delta (no buses were running) I had to walk 20 minutes in 28 degree weather with only my old tattered sport jacket on my back to keep me warm. Upon arrival in Salt Lake, I take my sports jacket off, go outside to the garbage can, and throw it away.

On Thursday night, after three days of jet-lag and not being able to sleep, I attend a 7:00 p.m. meeting, which I do not usually attend. Adrian chairs and he calls on all his friends the entire meeting.

I see Don, my sponsor the next day and tell him about the experience. This time, I tell him that I had kept my anger to myself instead of exploding all over Adrian and the rest of the group. I also tell my sponsor that it is ironic that I had attended a lot of other meetings where I did not share and did not get angry with the chair. I concluded that the only difference between Adrian's style and mine had to do with control. It was the loss of control that I did not like which allowed me to develop anger towards another human being. That was a big step for me.

The next day, after my morning meditations, I begin to feel enormous changes pour out of me. I cry and it hurts. I weep for everything that has happened in my life. I weep for others less fortunate than me. I want to love others for having loved me. I know that I have to let go of my past in order to make room for my future. I cry because I am no longer Superman, invincible, and all-knowing. I am beaten and scared.

Suddenly, I visualize the peeling of a soft, flaky croissant. My view of the world begins to get lighter, even among the dark-clouded skies of the Utah winter. I visualize a beautiful rose dying, letting its petals fall to the ground in slow motion. I knew that I had to trust God, let go and love myself again.

A lot of things happened that weekend:

- Scott shares that he remembers renting space underneath the Club, seeing people coming and going for months, and hearing the group end the meeting with the Serenity Prayer. He decides to check it out. After several months of coming to meetings, getting Newcomer chips, drinking and returning, he remembers telling the group that "I could build a house from the Newcomer chips that I had received in early days of sobriety." He then mentioned that a senior sober told him that he was wrong and that "You could build a coffin from all the chips that you had received." I sat silent, processed what he had just said, and found out later that Brent, my grand sponsor, had coined that phrase.

- Toby and I fought for hours. At one point I wouldn't even talk to her. Her tears and pleadings fell on silent ears. I had asked her for help because I could not continue to go to parties, movies, theatre, shopping, and hang out with people, places and things that would remind me of my old drinking habits.

- I attended four meetings and learned that there were very few AA birthdays in the month of December since many people do not become sober until after the holidays. I also learned that alcohol-related suicides jump in the month of December.

- I saw Saddam Hussein arrested on television and watched commentary for hours; everything else seeming trivial in comparison.

- I completed my 9th step and told my sponsor that I was doing my 10th, 11th and 12th steps daily. He looked at me and said, "At your next AA meetings I want you to raise your hand and tell people that you are available to be a temporary sponsor." I said I was not ready and that I wanted to have one year of sobriety under my belt. He told me to raise my hand. And, I responded, "Damn you."

After a good night's sleep, I go to a meeting and get asked to sponsor a 16 year-old named Cole. I call Don for advice and could not get through because his wife changed the home number and forgot to tell him. I called Bill, Brent, and Jennifer who offer me good advice. I hand Cole a "Big Book" and give him a small reading assignment. He agrees and commits to meeting me again in two days. Sadly, he shows up stoned and gets thrown out of Friendship Hall for smoking cigarettes at the meeting.

Early the next morning, Toby wakes me whispering that she wants me. She gets on top and makes love with passion that I have never known. Unfortunately, my alcoholic brain cannot stay in the moment. Terrible, sad, evil, painful thoughts from my past erupt with such velocity that I have to stop.

I could not tell what was going on but I felt afraid in the dark and that I was doing something wrong. I throw Toby off of me, lie still for minutes, and finally share with her my most intimate thoughts. I sit on the side of the bed and tell her, for the first time, a lot about my past experiences with prostitution. I tell her that many times I had gone to prostitutes for sex and would buy marijuana from them. In spilling my guts, I find myself quoting the "Big Book".

Toby cries in the darkened room. I offer her my apologies and ask her if I can make amends. She says that I did not hurt her and that she weeps for me. She thanks me for sharing and we hold each other silently for minutes. As time slowly clicks away, my terrible secrets from my past leave unescorted.

For the first time in my life, I realize why those 10+ years of time and money spent in therapy never completed the process. It seems so simple now. Therapy focuses on anger and not on fear, which is the predecessor to anger. Therapy focuses on worldly causes and outcomes. It does not deal with spirituality or God. Therapy focuses on others, such as my parents, and does not look at my side of the equation. All of my therapists encouraged me to give up the prostitutes but no one every told me to give up drinking and smoking.

I now realize that my intertwining of sex, dope, and alcohol allowed me to avoid everything in the world and kept me in my loneliness. It is only my spiritual program of recovery that has allowed me to see, for the first time, that I could not do it alone and that I need help from a Power greater than myself in order to break the never-ending battle to find peace.

That painful night freed me to go forward and share more about my past with the group. I chaired the 10:00 a.m. Sunday meeting and shared secrets that I had kept inside me for more than 30 years. After my lead, I listened to other members talk about their families and how difficult this time of year was on them. Many could not cope with the stress of the holidays, their jobs and families, and as a result, did not return to meetings.

After several months of avoiding parties and events, Toby and I go to Cindy and John's. As I enter the house, the first thing I see is the bar; all stocked with the best liquors and wines. To my surprise I do not feel like drinking and want to share with everyone my sobriety. I lasted 4 hours.

I watch one guy who wants to make sure that everyone's glass is filled. I could see myself in him because I rarely drank alone, always wanted to drink with someone else and bought drinks for anyone who would spend time with me. In looking back, I was not a big man. In fact, I was nothing more than a wealthy socialite, A Gentleman Drunk, who could afford to bring others down to my level.

Later that night, as I drive home sober, I no longer feel sad for other drinkers and acknowledge that they will do whatever they want with their lives. The day after Christmas, I awake to a snowy morning and head over to a meeting, tugging my Chanukah menorah. At the meeting, I light all 8 candles in front of everyone. To my surprise, many ask about the Jewish holiday and let me watch my candles burn slowly as they share about Christmas.

Outside I see it snowing without an end in sight. Driving out of the parking lot I did a 180, stopped the car, got outside, and saw that a nail had punctured my front left tire. I immediately thought of another Club member who had been working at the Club, performing a lot of repairs. In my heart and soul, I knew it was a single nail that he probably misplaced. Miraculously, I made it home, took a warm bath, prayed a lot, and forgave the stranger who got me to see the true meaning of the holidays — forgiveness, compassion, love and acceptance.

The days after Christmas were brutal. My brain was on fire and I could not get rid of the pain. The everlasting memory of my car skidding out of control and the fact the nails had come from the construction at the Club pissed me off.

Toby and I had drag-down fights over every little thing. I would lose hours on end as I felt despair and suicide. Skies were dark and there was snow everywhere. To make matters worse, the snow plow blocked me in my own driveway.

Over Christmas and New Years I felt terrible anger and depression. I told my doctor that I could not longer handle my responsibilities without some anti-depressants. My sponsor agreed, and I started taking 20 mgs of Celexa.

Dad had two more mini-strokes and we all prayed that he would die.

On Jan. 2, Don changed the room format at the Club in order to make space for potential newcomers and posted several signs with messages about our Creator. I did not like the fact that he took away the old familiar environment which encouraged conversation and replaced it with a cold, austere, churchlike environment which minimized eye contact.

For an entire month, I studied Greek and Roman mythology in order to get a better understanding of how former generations viewed God. I would spend hours upon end on the Internet and report my findings to the Club members. Many members came over to me and told me to stop analyzing God and accept the fact that He is in control and that I should simply have "Blind Faith."

We get to the end of January. I start galloping with vigor, energy, love, compassion, and concern. I begin to socialize again, recognize that I am not able to save anyone, and that people can be saved if they turn to God for help.

I theorize that my brain is like a sponge and that I was able to absorb alcohol all those years until my sponge got full.

It was not my fault nor could I have prevented it. All I can do now is stop it from happening to me again.

In one meeting, Susan says that happiness and money can coexist. She explains that happiness is an emotion and that money is an outside event. One can be happy and rich or one can be happy and poor. The two are not interlocked as I had previously believed.

In Los Angeles, I attend an AA meeting, after walking from my hotel to a church, which is strangely occupied by a Korean funeral. I go down to the basement and listen to Leo, a Jewish transplant from New York. Leo drives me back to my hotel and picks me up the next night to join him and his friends for Chinese food and a 50 + person stag meeting called "The White Flag."

Back at my hotel, I call Salt Lake City and listen to my Voice Mail. Carol, my mother's personal assistant, calls to tell me that Mom had a stroke. Jill, my sister, flies down for the weekend and calls. She slowly tells me that Mom fell in the hospital after a nurse put her in a chair without support and that Mom is completely paralyzed on one side of the body but can still talk.

A day later we learn that Mom has another setback caused by excess swelling at the brain stem. Lizzann, my ex-wife, Jordana, my oldest daughter, and Jill convene at the Hospital to watch my comatose mother.

The doctor tells the family that Mom's stroke has been caused by a clot which grew and cut off circulation to her brain. We are informed that she is unable to think or feel yet can still breathe on her own. After family concurrence, the doctor removes her feeding tube. Although she is brain dead, she continues to sleep comfortably; totally unaware of her environment. The doctor gives her 7 to 10 days to live.

Toby and I fly back to Salt Lake City from New York, and I receive my 9-month chip. I share a lot about my AA life and how I owe AA everything for keeping me sober. My eyes swell as I look around the room and see Toby crying. Even will all the good things that are happening in my sobriety, I cannot stop thinking about Mom.

Chapter 13
(January 2004 – April 2004 - Months 9-12)

THANK YOU, GOD

The doctor has removed Mom's feeding tube and she is quickly starving to death. He tells us that she does not feel any pain; uncharacteristically, I do.

Words do not adequately describe death. Years ago, my therapist told me that we get angry at people who die when they leave us behind. Prior to my alcoholic recovery I would have been angry with both Mom and God and drank to get rid of the pain. Instead, I now pray for guidance.

It was Thursday morning, January 29th, 2004, two months before Mom's 74th birthday. I awake early to take the garbage out. While browsing the net, I see that James Brown has been arrested in South Carolina for beating his wife.

The telephone rings. I answer. It's Jill. She simply says, "Mom's gone." I feel nothing. I say nothing.

Without expressing any deep emotion, she asks me if Toby and I can fly to Florida that afternoon so that we can bury Mom the next morning. I lose my cool and tell her that she's rushing it and does not understand what it takes to drop everything and fly across the country. She counters with her anger and tells me that the rest of the family is already there and that they have been watching Mom die for the last 10 days. I tell Jill to "have the funeral without me" and give Toby the phone.

Minutes pass. I run around the room in circles, ranting and complaining about Jill. Toby watches silently until I finally compose myself. Toby signals me to make the call.

I first call Delta, my preferred airline. They quote me $1200/person to fly to Ft. Lauderdale through Atlanta. My anger resurfaces.

Then I call Jet Blue, whom I have never flown, and they want $800/person to fly to West Palm through New York.

Finally, I get onto Orbitz and find a same day $330/person RT fare to West Palm on American Airlines through Dallas. Since American Airlines uses the same initials as Alcoholics Anonymous, I look up at the sky and thank God for his guidance.

Toby and I have 45 minutes to make the 12:00 flight. Amazingly, we pack, water the plants, shut down the heating and water, cancel appointments, reschedule dinner arrangements, touch base with clients, leave for the airport, and make the flight.

After takeoff, I look out the window and see banners waving in the sky. Upon further inspection, I feel the presence of all my dead relatives. After a double take, I see Mom's spirit flying along side the plane. For the first time in her life, she is happy and at peace. I lean over, kiss Toby, and tell her that I love her.

In less than 12 hours from the time we received the phone call we were in the Boca Raton Marriott awaiting the funeral, which would be held the next day at 1:00 p.m.

We awake at 6:00 a.m. Both of us are on auto-pilot. I feel numb. I pray constantly repeating God's name, asking for guidance. I feel a nervous energy permeating throughout my body.

I get on the Internet and find an e-mail from one of my readers who points me to the Boca Raton AA website. I jot down the Pompano morning meeting address and tell Toby that I'm going to a meeting.

Toby and I prepare for the funeral. My sister calls to tell me that the rabbi told her to tell me to write down my thoughts. I tell her that AA encourages me to talk from my heart.

Toby and I go over to Starbucks. After coffee, she walks back to the hotel while I drive down to Pompano to attend the Bottom Line Group.

Lots of smiling faces fill a large room facing Sample Road. Since it's an open meeting, I share about my fears, anxieties and concerns about the funeral. After the meeting several people come over, offer help, and give me their telephone numbers.

At 12:00 P.M. Toby and I are the first to arrive at the funeral home. We are shown into a large pink-brown room that is unsparingly filled with beautifully decorated Kleenex boxes.

For an hour we sit at the end of the room, greet people and talk about Mom, who is in an open casket next door. When I am not talking to guests, I look around the room and see my two daughters, Jordana and Moira, Lizzann, my ex-wife, Jill, my sister, and Benoit, her ex-husband.

We are then ushered into the funeral chapel. The "rent-a-rabbi" talks briefly about Mom and the family. Following the rabbi, two of Mom's friends, Ruthie and Barbara, talk briefly about how they felt about Mom. Jill then takes the stage with her prepared speech. Although I could make out her words, it was difficult to hear her through her choked, tearful voice.

Finally, it's my turn. I walk to the stage with confidence and assurance that what I am about to say is from my heart. I slowly speak looking at everyone in the room, peeling off memories of Mom and Dad.

I tell our guests that my life has changed since I found out that I was an alcoholic and voluntarily committed myself to an alcoholic recovery program. As a result of the program, I shared how I had changed from blaming my parents to taking responsibility. I talked about 9-stepping Mom, that we had started a beautiful journey to first base, and that I was sorry that I did not know why God had taken her at this moment in my life.

I quoted the Bible and Genesis and talked about where God says "Let Us Create Mankind in Our Own Image." I basically said to the audience, "Who was God talking to when He said this?" I suggested that He was talking to angels and that we all had our own individual angels looking after us.

People cried, laughed, and smiled. Many came over to me as we awaited our ride to the cemetery. They told me how proud Mom was of my accomplishment. I smiled, thanked them, and told them that Mom loved my speech.

Several cars jogged into line and turned on their lights. While heading to the cemetery, Lenny and Jeanie, two of my parent's closest friends, told us about the time when Mom drank without eating and fell asleep in front of everyone - a story that I could relate to.

Jill stressed because the police escort never showed and locals kept honking their horns at the slow procession. At one point, the lead driver had to get out of his car and motion uninvited cars out of our line.

We arrive at the mausoleum. As we enter the massive structure we see beautiful granite-laced plaques with the names of other departed Jews. The pure white room warms even the coldest heart as you admire the ivory-rose sun-drenched walls.

The rabbi says Kaddish while family members pour Israeli sand over the casket.

Toby and I go back to the hotel, fall asleep, miss dinner, and wake up late to talk about the beautiful ceremony. Although the skies had been threatening, it never rained and, for that, I am forever grateful.

The next day, Toby and I go over to Whitehall to tell Dad that Mom has passed away. As we enter Dad's room, his eyes are slightly opened. I ask Elizabeth, his day nurse, to leave the room. I then lean over, grab his hand, and tell him about my sobriety and Mom. He lays lifeless and does not respond. I feel that I'm looking into a one-way mirror without any reflection and realize that he is trapped inside of a tortured body.

Back at the house, Lenny shares with me a story about Dad. He tells me that when Dad had his first stroke he asked Lenny to help him kill himself and that Lenny turned him down. Lenny's story made sense because I knew Dad never liked people in wheel chairs and always frowned upon people less fortunate then him.

For the first time in my life, I saw Dad as a weak person and not as strong as I thought. I had always believed that he remained on this planet because he did not want to die. After hearing Lenny's story, I came to believe that Dad was alive in that 13-year debilitating condition because God wanted him to stay.

After several weeks, Toby and I were scheduled to go to Florida to spend our first weekend with Mom at her house. With her passing, I had no desire to get on an airplane. In fact, I had nightmares and told Toby that I could not do it. So, she cashed in some miles, went by herself and stayed with Celeste and John, good friends who live north of Palm Beach.

Meanwhile, I continue to go to meetings and share my sorrows. In Chicago, I meet Jane who tells me that she is a former editor of an encyclopedia and has more than 25 years of sobriety in the program. Naturally, I ask her to assist me with this book and she accepts.

As my sobriety birthday approaches, I decide to throw a gigantic sobriety party on the Sunday after my 1-year anniversary. Toby tells me that my oldest daughter, Jordana, plans to fly out and that my youngest daughter, Moira, cannot come due to her school schedule.

My sobriety feels good. Yet, I feel lost. Although I enjoy the meetings, I find myself laughing at other's sharing about things that I also experienced; like getting thrown into jail, having my drinking privileges stopped on the airlines, and misusing money.

I listen to newcomers and many of them do not stay, complaining that they cannot relate to us, and I understand.

People point out that I am arrogant, too honest with people about their problems, and that I should be more understanding of others. Today, I listened to a lady who has been in the program three years and was bitching about the program, her life, her children's lives and that she wants to kill her daughter's husband. I told her to kill herself and stop wasting my time.

I still have a hard time when I am alone. Although I do not feel the need to drink, I feel the urge to do something more productive than reading recovery books, watching television, working out, cleaning out closets, straightening out my room, and preparing for clients. I continue to study alcoholism and know very little about the subject.

I know that I am on the right track but I miss the old days of getting wasted. Life seemed so simple then. Yet, I know that I have the uncanny ability to forget about the crap I went through and the problems which I personally created.

It's now 3:00 A.M. Wednesday, March 3. I cannot sleep. I am restless and do not understand what's happening to me. I am in the process of completing a second 4th step with my sponsor, which is customary to do before a recovery birthday.

Although there are fewer items on my list, none of them are the same as my last 4th step back in July, 2003. My sponsor tells me that's O.K. He tells me that as one emotionally matures, and begins to truly feel and reflect recovery, the list evolves and changes to reflect new thoughts yet undiscovered.

Don comes over to my house to review my 4th step. Toby drives out of the house without seeing his car parked in the driveway. She hits Don's car which rolls into the street. Don's car had $2200 in damage while Toby's SUV had $3300. We paid the deductibles and made Don whole on his car. It was a very expensive 4th step.

I meet a woman from France on the porch of the club who has difficulty expressing herself in English. I have been selected to help translate. She is saying "Je suis perdue" which means "I am lost."

I also meet her alcoholic friend, Guy, who I help with his resume. One day Guy asks me to become his sponsor. At this point, he is my second sponsee. He tells me about an incident where he was so drunk in the hospital that he pulled out his IV and spurted blood all over the room.

Earlier today I learned that Bill W. talked about the 12 steps in his own story on pages 12-13 of the "Big Book". I am amazed that I have read the same story more than 30 times and have never seen the connection.

My sister e-mails me and brings me up-to-date on Mom's estate and Dad's assets. She is upset that the portfolio has substantially declined over the last three years due to the recession and Mom's withdrawals. She comforts herself, nonetheless, with the knowledge that the portfolio has survived and is still intact. I remind her that life is good and that she should be proud of herself for balancing her own life and taking care of Mom and Dad for the last 13 years.

For several weeks, I attend many AA meetings. Usually I listen. But often I have to say something to say to people who, I think, are not working the program well. My mind forecasts their relapse and there is nothing I can say or do to stop them from going out for another drink.

Several months go by and each event seems to take on more importance as my 1-year anniversary approaches:

- Don, my sponsor, tells me that he and his wife are splitting
- Brent, one of my good AA buddies, secretly takes my name off the birthday board thinking I would find it funny; I did not.

- Valter, my restaurant friend, calms me down after a drunk tries to punch me in the parking lot.
- Guy and I disagree on a major issue and I tell him that I can no longer be his sponsor.
- Patty, a woman at the Club, tells all of us that the landowner has sold out to a major developer and wants us to vacate the Club.

My East Coast AA friends suggest that I attend "too many" meetings and that I should cut back or even drop out of AA. I test the waters and write an article in my newsletter about leaving AA. Hell breaks lose as more than 50 readers e-mail me their opinion.

I check out Moderation Management and find out that they have rules also; no more than 14 drinks a week, no more than 1 drink per hour, 1 glass of water required between drinks, no drinking two days in a row, etc.

I go onto other addiction websites and find out that there are others who were AA members who left the program yet remained sober. Unfortunately, they also have rules and I do not like most of them.

I finally conclude that alcoholics, including myself, love to drink for effect. To moderate or limit the number of drinks defeats the purpose. So, I figure if I cannot drink what I want, when I want, I might as well stay sober.

Ultimately, I decide to stay with the program, albeit attending fewer meetings.

On Saturday, April 3, I go out to Antelope Island and see adult seagulls training their young. I talk to the birds as they fly over and none pay attention to me. I drive around the Island and see some buffalo. One of them stands alone from the rest of the pack. Like him, I feel alone.

I attend a Saturday night meeting and we have a brownout. Instead of canceling the meeting, the group takes out candles and continues to read from the "Big Book" under candlelight. The lights flicker as they try to relight themselves. There was no doubt in my mind that God was there helping us to find the light.

One of the Club members becomes unruly after several meetings. No one knows why. We all hypothesize that his meds may have been altered. Several members speak to him and his wife. Twice he has to be removed from the premises. Ultimately, the Club has to sanction him. I have not seen him since he was removed by the police.

As my sobriety birthday approaches, I am wired 24 hours a day. I work with Don, sponsor, club manager and now caterer-to-the-stars, and review details with military precision.

My eldest daughter, Jordana, flies in from North Carolina. She is now a senior at Wake Forest and I proudly show her off to my friends. She exudes charm and clearly demonstrates complete confidence in herself. She hands me a book, *Why A Daughter Needs A Dad*. I open the book and see the following inscription:

April 15, 2004
Daddy,

I am <u>so</u> proud of you! Congratulations on one amazing year.

I love you,
Jordana

On Saturday morning, Jordana and I go over to pick up my newly-acquired, 65,000 mile used BMW red convertible, which Brent, who has apologized, sold me.

I awake early on Sunday, April 18th, the day of my party. The skies are overcast. I go on the Internet and see a snow advisory. The outside temperature is 37 degrees.

Toby hands me a gift box. I open it and see a beautiful diamond-encrusted bracelet with the inscription April 15, 2003; the day I stopped drinking.

Jordana, Toby, and I head over to the Club. I see Don and desperately need to talk to him. He calms me down and tells me that everything will go well and that I need to trust God. I tell him that God is testing me and that He likes to upset me. Don smiles and laughs.

Ten minutes into the meeting, I approach the front of the room to receive my 1-year chip. Although I do not remember the exact words, I talked about the Power Tools of the program (concept by Brent), planning one's life without expectation (concept by Susan), and God's creating the world in 6 days. I further elaborated that most religious theologians believe that the Bible's interpretation of 6 days equates to 6 billion days as we know it. Therefore, when people tell me that I am not living in the moment, I remind them that I do live my life one day at a time. It's on God time, not mine or theirs.

Jordana and I take the BMW out to the desert and I teach her how to drive a stick shift. She has difficulty getting the car started and tells me that maybe we are in 3rd gear and not 1st. She is correct. She shifts into first, hits the gas, releases the clucth and tools down the highway access road at a comfortable 70 MPH. I keep looking at her and thrill at her smiles.

My sister and I receive Mom's life insurance. Within a couple of weeks I pay off remaining credit card debts, insurance loans and our home mortgage. With additional funds, Toby and I buy a second home in Scottsdale in order to get out of the Utah winters, which we have endured for 10 years.

At the party, I pass around the Chips that I received over the last couple of days. Tammy drops one in her drink. She and I look at each other as if she had just killed my best friend.

Throughout the day, I receive numerous thanks from all of my old and new friends. Many call in from New York or e-mail me from all over the world. I take each phone call and thank them graciously for tolerating me all those years, expressing my love.

As the party slows down, and few remain, I go into the living room, sit down at the Steinway and present my most recent composition.

Why Not Try God?
Music and Lyrics
By
Jeffrey Taylor © Copyright April 2004 All Rights Reserved

I've read the Big Book
At least a dozen times
Each time I read it
I read between the lines
Now that I'm sober
At least a full year
What can I tell you
To make you drop your beer?
Step 1 – I am lost
Step 2 – I'm not boss
Step 3 – Why not try God?
Step 4 – Make a list
Step 5 – Share my piss
Step 6 – Why not try God?
Everything I tried, turned to shit
Miracles come to those with wit
Why not try God?
I've read the 12 & 12
At least a dozen times
Each time I read it
I think about my crimes
Now that I'm sober
For once in my life
What can I tell you
To help you with your strife?

Step 7 – Press delete
Step 8 – Spread a sheet
Step 9 – Why not try God?
Step 10 – Apologize
Step 11 – Philosophize
Step 12 – Why not try God?
Life is not bad, cause of AA
With your free time, for me you should pray
Why not try God?
Why not try God?

As I finish my song, people come over and tell me that it's good enough for Broadway, and that I should write a musical about alcoholism.

Who knows what God has in store for me? I know that if I pray daily for guidance, I will find the answers.

I also know that I don't have to rush since I have the rest of my "sober" life to figure it out. Thank you for listening and with that I'll take another 24.